In the thirty-two years I was a college coach I witnessed first-hand how young men were coming to college with the lack of a spiritual foundation that would prepare them for life's next set of challenges. You could tell that Godly parenting skills were sorely missing. Dr. Eric Mason in his book, *Manhood Restored* helps men regain their leadership role in the family. I would recommend this book to any father or husband who desires to step up to the challenge presented by Dr. Mason.

—Tommy Bowden, ESPN analyst and
veteran college football coach

I have been a friend and fan of Dr. Eric Mason for over a decade. I could not be more excited about his voice speaking into what I believe is the most critical issue of our day, the state of our men. *Manhood Restored* is a powerful resource that will help men of all ages understand the problems men create and how they can get on the solution side. The ideas and truths in this book are not just detached ideals written from an ivory tower . . . I have watched Eric work out his own masculinity in a powerful way as a husband, father, church planter, church leader, movement leader, and good friend.

—Dr. John W. Bryson, cofounder,
Pastor Fellowship Memphis and
lead writer, Co-Presenter 33 the Series

Eric Mason has written a practical, biblical, and gospel-centered vision of true manhood. Saturated in the person and work of the Lord Jesus Christ, our perfect model of true manhood, Mason carefully addresses an essential key to changing our churches and communities—the discipleship of men. Read this book, brother, and watch the Lord change your life. Share it and watch the Lord change the brothers in your sphere of influence.

—H. B. Charles Jr., pastor/teacher at the Shiloh
Metropolitan Baptist Church, Jacksonville, Florida

Sin is social. Even the most private and individual of sins—wallowing in porn, for example—are never merely individual. Devouring porn may be an individual offense, but it is also an insult to God—and because it works out in perverted or abusive or manipulative relationships, it is also social. That is why the gospel, in all its massive power, does not only reconcile us to God, but so transforms us that healthy relationships begin to bud all around us: the shattered social fabric begins to be healed. Perhaps no human relationships are more broken today than those within the family, within what used to be the family. And most frightening of all are the sad realities bound up with absent or abusive or selfish fathers. I gratefully applaud the ministry of Eric Mason as he seeks to apply the whole counsel of God to form Christian men, Christian husbands, Christian fathers, who in gospel grace and joy take up the reins of responsibility and faithful service to stamp new generations with a passion for strong, self-sacrificing love and holiness.

—D. A. Carson, research professor of New Testament at Trinity Evangelical Seminary in Deerfield, Illinois

Pastor Eric Mason is a man I have known and respected for many years. He has planted and is leading a fast growing Bible teaching city reaching church in a rough Philly neighborhood. I'm excited to see this book released as it blends his rare skill set as a first rate formally trained theologian who is literally on the front lines of urban ministry.

—Mark Driscoll, founding pastor of Mars Hill Church, Founder of The Resurgence, cofounder of Acts 29, *New York Times* #1 best-selling author

In this age of increasing confusion about manhood, marriage and God's Word, Eric Mason has emerged as a refreshing, clear and prophetic voice. This book not only speaks to today's urban youth, it also powerfully speaks to all who have concerns about the general direction of our society. For anyone cares about applying God's truth to contemporary challenges, *Manhood Restored* is a must reed.

—Dr. Carl Ellis Jr., Assistant Professor of Practical Theology Redeemer Seminary

Manhood has fallen on hard times. So many men have been beaten-up by the past, mired in the consequences of bad choices, and confused and disoriented by a culture committed to redefining manhood so that we can cover the fractures and disguise the torment. That's why I am thrilled for the gift of *Manhood Restored*. What a clear, compelling portrait of the power of the gospel to transform broken males into whole, godly men. You have pointed us to the Savior who makes all things new. This is our hope and our courage.

—Dr. Crawford W. Loritts Jr., author, speaker, radio host, and senior pastor of Fellowship Bible Church in Roswell, Georgia

Few issues fire me up like the topic of men acting like men. My friend and ministry partner Eric Mason offers hope to, incites healing for, and wreaks havoc on men. Every man who follows Jesus needs to read this book and apply the biblical truth in it to his life. The men in our churches, the marriages in our churches, and our churches will be better for it.

—James MacDonald, Senior Pastor of Harvest Bible Chapel and author of *Vertical Church*

There is no greater need in our day than to answer two questions: What is a man? and What is a godly man? In this helpful and biblical book, Eric Mason answers these questions. If you are a man, read and heed this great work.

—Dr. Darrin Patrick, lead pastor of The Journey, St. Louis, Missouri, and author of *For the City, Church Planter: The Man, The Message, The Mission,* and A *Dude's Guide to Manhood: Finding True Manliness in a World Of Counterfeits*

As parents of three boys, we are praying that each will live God honoring lives, realize their God-given potential and reach their God-given destiny. This will only happen if a clear course—a map of manhood—is drawn out for them to follow. *Manhood Restored* is a tool that will not only help grown men live well but also serve as a compass for the next generation. Our friend Eric Mason writes from experience. We've admired him as a faithful husband and father, disciplined student of God's Word and dedicated servant of the Lord. His integrity and wisdom shine through on every page. Men of all ages should read this book and treasure its truths deeply in their souls.

—Jerry and Priscilla Shirer, Bible teacher and author

From the moment God formed man, we were charged with reflecting God's essence and reflecting His character. Throughout history, this intended role of a man has gradually shifted to a view that's now become common—the notion that a man's merit is predicated on his worldly success, by all means. We have become consumed with being THE man instead of A man.

True "Manhood" has lost the real prerequisite, an intimate relationship with God! A team captain cannot effectively lead without being a reflection of the coach. When men re-establish our connection with our creator, we see the fruit—healthier families, stronger communities, a society with substance, and world leaders who are equipped with integrity and purpose.

—Allan Houston, New York Knicks

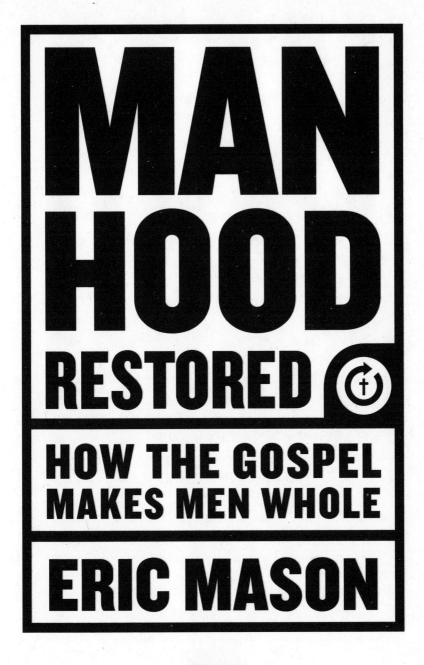

MAN HOOD RESTORED

HOW THE GOSPEL MAKES MEN WHOLE

ERIC MASON

B&H
PUBLISHING GROUP
NASHVILLE, TENNESSEE

Published by B&H Publishing Group
Nashville, Tennessee

Dewey Decimal Classification: 248.842
Subject Heading: CHRISTIAN LIFE \ MEN \
DISCIPLESHIP

2 3 4 5 6 7 8 • 17 16 15 14 13

This book is dedicated to memory of my mother, Florence G. Mason. Who sacrificed years for me to be educated and pointed to Jesus in the harsh and challenging realities of the inner city of Washington, DC. Rest Eternally 1924–2012

CONTENTS

ACKNOWLEDGMENTS

I want to thank the living God for restoring me to Him. I am so thankful for Your commitment to me in Jesus. I am forever grateful for Your eternal investment in my soul.

Thank you to my wife, Yvette, for your friendship and sacrifice to be married to me. I adore you and count it beyond an honor for us to be together. To my boys, Immanuel and Nehemiah, I pray that your eyes will find their way to these pages and find hope in them. I love you both more than words can express. Thanks to my family for allowing me the time and energy to write this book.

Epiphany Fellowship: I love you guys more than you'll ever know. As God's undershepherd to you, I have written this work with you in mind. Let's take Philly by storm.

To LifeWay: You guys know what you are doing and I am grateful for you. Thank you for believing in me, and what God has placed in me, and drawing it out. Ed Stetzer, thank you for putting me on LifeWay's radar. Jedidiah Coppenger, Brian Daniel, Phillip Nation, and the rest of the staff, thanks for being easy to work with. Your encouragement has been a blessing.

FOREWORD
BY DR. TONY EVANS

Those who know me are acutely aware of my passion for men's ministry. Whether it is speaking at a Promise Keepers meeting, a men's retreat, or a men's breakfast, you can regularly find me heavily engaged in ministry to men. This is because most of the devolution of our contemporary culture can be traced directly to the brokenness of men today. Whether the issue is faithfulness, crime, poverty, or a myriad of other social ills; at the core is the failure of men to become what God has created them to be.

While there are many reasons for this failure, the pain left behind of broken hearts, dreams, families, and communities is obvious to all. Unless there is a restoration of biblical manhood we can ill expect there to be restoration of an ordered society. Unless the church begins to take lead in seriously prioritizing men's ministry and discipling this and the next generation of men, then we are doomed to see the further decay of our society. If the saga of a nation is the saga of its families written large, then the saga of a family is the saga of its men written large. Just as God found it difficult to find a man to save the culture from destruction in Ezekiel's day, so now He is still finding it the exception to find man as He defines them today.

That is why this fine work by one of my sons in the ministry is so timely. *Manhood Restored* may best be defined as a "theology of manhood." Eric Mason does a masterful job of unearthing the biblical teaching of the Creator's intent in creating men. He allows the Scriptures to define, instruct, guide, and clarify the true meaning of manhood.

In a day when the definition of manhood is up for grabs by a culture that has exited from the Creator's intent, *Manhood Restored* gives anyone who is seriously desirous of knowing what real manhood is supposed to look like a solid place to go.

Because Eric is a pastor, he does not write this book in abstract esoteric terms so that the reader is left in a theological jog wondering where to go and what to do next. *Manhood Restored* will inspire, challenge, encourage, and educate you on God's gift of manhood. Eric recognizes all too well the challenges men face today, the pain so many men hide, the emptiness so many men endure, the vices so many men escape too, and the anger so many men display. Therefore this work is designed to make men better, not simply analyzing and criticizing their failures.

Manhood Restored will enable all who read it to begin the process of becoming what their divine birthright has destined them to be while equipping them to help other men as well.

Dr. Tony Evans

Senior Pastor, Oak Cliff Bible Fellowship

President, The Urban Alternative

FOREWORD
BY MATT CHANDLER

My dad has a great heart. Although he is a large, burly man whom some find "scary," he loves to laugh, cries easily, and loves my children with zeal. When I watch him at family gatherings and talk with him in other settings, I always come away in awe of the power of the gospel.

My father grew up in an abusive home where neglect was the preference to the physical violence he routinely received. It was an awful upbringing and one he swore to himself he wouldn't unleash on his own family one day. This environment created cavernous holes in his heart and his development as a man; he feared rejection, hated himself, and could easily feel disrespected and fly into a rage. He filled those holes with alcohol and promiscuity and quickly developed an addiction to both of those along with his anger. As a father of three, I have to believe that when my dad first held me he promised himself he would be a better dad to his son than his dad and stepdads were to him. He gave it a good go, but in the end his hate for himself was too strong and our home started to, in many ways, mirror the environment he grew up in. When I was a kid, my dad could be a lot of fun in one moment and could turn violent in the next. With the temperature of our house constantly and rapidly changing, I felt as though it was my fault and set out to try and please and help my dad love me. The wounds he had were creating wounds in me. The insecurity he felt began to be imprinted on me, his rage was becoming my rage, his lusts my lusts until Jesus decided this was over.

I heard and received the gospel of Jesus Christ a few days before my eighteenth birthday. It was like warm water on my soul. To be approved and loved by God despite me was an overwhelming truth to a young man that longed for approval and love. I learned quickly that despite my love for Jesus I was banged up, bruised, and continued in some of my boyish ways instead of becoming all that God would have me be as a man. As I continued to marinate in the gospel of Jesus Christ and the Father's approval of me in Jesus, slowly I began to change. I was set free to serve, risk, be vulnerable, and take on responsibility without fear of failure, which led me to work harder but not to be approved but because I was approved. My father came to know Jesus several years ago now, and I am watching this same gospel work, heal, and transform him.

Eric Mason has served us well with this book. To give us pragmatic steps alone would be insufficient and in the end unhelpful. Our souls are broken. To put gas in a car that doesn't run is an exercise in futility. Eric starts where we all must start, the power of the gospel to heal us and transform us into what we were created for. He doesn't stop there and ends the book powerfully on what the gospel empowers us to do. Read this slowly and prayerfully. Its bold, fearless, Scripture saturated, truth-telling pages might just be used by the Spirit of God to take you into a new season of fulfillment and maturity in your understanding what it means to be a man.

Christ is All,

Matt Chandler

Lead Pastor, The Village Church

President of Acts 29 Church Planting Network

PREFACE

I have written this book because men need to know that only through the gospel of Jesus Christ can they be what God intends. My prayer is that this book and the accompanying curriculum would help scores of men, old and young, to see God's great purpose for them in Jesus. My prayer is that churches will find this book to be a catalyst and a primer for the intentional development of men. I pray it would find its way into Sunday schools, small groups, and bedside tables, so that from the corner office to the street corner men find all they need in Jesus. May disciples of men be made and lives saved.

Introduction

 Another book on manhood? I can only imagine that's what you thought as you read the title. There is a pantheon of books on the topic, so why another one? Legitimate question. I know other books on the subject I've read have made phenomenal contributions to my own soul and shaped my understanding of God's purpose for manhood. My hope is that this work will add something to these other contributions that is inseparable from seeing God's true purpose in manhood—the undeniable thread of the gospel.

I would, in fact, say that we don't have enough material written on manhood. I base that on the fact that our gender continues to be steeped in a crisis of identity—genocide, self-preservation, spiritual anemia, role disillusionment, absence, perpetual adolescence, and emotional immaturity. We are deeply deficient in understanding and practicing how to relate to God and others in a healthy way.

We need the gospel. We need it more than books. More than studies. More than groups. We need the life-giving, identity-establishing, purpose-defining gospel of Jesus Christ.

Men can have covenants, documents, strategies, and pragmatic principles, but without the gospel there is no authentic empowerment to execute what is laid out in them. The goal of this book is not to motivate men with guilt of their failures but to facilitate an undeniable encounter with the ultimate God-man. The hero of manhood for this work will be the incarnate Jesus Christ. The eternal contribution of Jesus has changed the course of manhood forever.

We will peruse the beginning, seeing God's original intent for manhood as displayed in the differences between men and women. We will see the divine nature of God displayed in those differences. Although there are aspects of unanimity, we will seek to see how God created men and women as different masterpieces in the landscape of His creation. Understanding God's design in creation will help us further explore the unique portrait of each man as an equal, yet different and distinct image bearer of the glory of God on Earth.

But as we'll see, something went terribly wrong. The fall broke us all, and the systemic issues in our culture are a degeneration of that fall. Being that all creation has been cursed (Rom. 8:22), man lives in a state of death in the midst of this cursed creation. Whereas we were created to represent God's reign in creation, we continue to invent ways to deepen our separation from God by rejecting Him in every area of our lives.

We sense this separation—the void between what we are and what we know, somewhere inside of us, we could and should be. Men have tried to bridge the gap by constructing our own ideas of what it means to "really be a man." Whether the businessman, the thug, the rapper, the athlete, the playboy, or the bishop, these cultural caricatures fall drastically short of God's intent for a man.

But the biggest, and scariest, challenge that has emanated from the fall involves fatherhood. My close friend Blake Wilson describes this plague as "Daddy Deprivation." The crisis in fatherhood crosses cultural and socioeconomic grounds; it's a crisis prevalent in all areas of society, for the absence of a father leaves a lasting void in a man's identity and development.

Because of the deprivation of fathers, we see human efforts as unredeemed replacements. Unredeemed determination, womanizing, being a better father than their father, bitterness, and all the rest can't fill the gap of a father. All replacements are illegitimate means for a legitimate need (Jer. 1:11–13). We need fathers, and we're only going to be fathers to our children when we see that true fatherhood is rooted and defined in God the Father.

That examination will bring us to the beginnings of the redemption of manhood. Jesus—the second, new, and better Adam—is lifted before us as the ultimate portrait of what it means to be a man. Manhood is core and fundamental to the identity of Jesus, before and after He walked on the earth. Throughout the Old Testament, we see glimpses of the perfect Man establishing Himself as the hope for all generations. Understanding this sets the stage for what we see from Jesus throughout the gospel—that His manhood was rooted in His understanding of His existence as connected to God as Father and His call to courageously sacrifice His life for us. It was the gospel that drove Jesus' manhood in His incarnation, and that manhood pleased the Father greatly.

Even today His example of what it means to be a man is powerful to show men today how to care for the people God has given to us. Although no man is Jesus, men must have lives in Christ that purposefully ruin people for the glory of God. Real men follow Jesus and fulfill their purpose in their generation (Acts 13:36). After the death, resurrection, and ascension of Jesus, Christians are part of a "newmanity" unlike the humanity destroyed by the fall.

As Paul articulated in Ephesians 2:15, Christ has created one new man in Himself, and this newmanity is made up of men and women of different ethnicities and time periods. Within this, the males within the newmanity have been restored to God's new eternal intentions in Jesus Christ. As a part of God's new community, men play a vital role in leading in the home and in the church. We will look at a vast array of characteristics of what the gospel has produced in this new community.

Our exploration will take us into key practical areas where manhood is vitally needed, places where men have failed over the centuries: Sexuality, the home, the church, and other societal institutions are crying out for real men of the newmanity to rise up and lead.

From beginning to end, God has a purpose for men. It's a purpose that's been lost but, in and through Jesus Christ, one that might yet be recovered. It's time for manhood to be restored.

CHAPTER 1

The Life and Death of Manhood

 In an interview with Bryan "Baby" Williams, leader of the Young Money Cash Money Billionaires, a question was raised about the term *bling, bling*. This term is a colloquialism used first in hip-hop culture to speak about the mass accumulation of material wealth. In this culture, every time there is an accomplishment that leads to gaining more wealth, "bling, bling" is announced to self and others as a way of saying that more has been brought into one's possession. In regard to the term, Baby stated, "I wish we would have trademarked that phrase cause we originated it. People would have to pay us every time they used the term and it would trace them back to us" [paraphrase].

That's how trademarking works. It's a claim on something original, something unique, that establishes ownership. Many might use, build on, or add something to the original, but the trademark establishes the absolute first origin of something. It's important in business; it's more important in creation.

God holds the trademark on creation. More specifically, God holds the trademark on manhood. All of God's creation was brought into being with a sense of care and love, but when He created man He didn't speak him into existence as He did the stars, water, land, and animals. Instead God innovated a new technique in creation. God *formed* man. This term is rich in depth and meaning—God handmade man by sculpting Him from what He had already created.

Formed means "fashioned, shaped, or forged, usually by plan or design."[1] The term implies an intentionality; forming isn't haphazard. To *form* is to devise, prepare, i.e., think about future actions with a particular plan of action as an extension of forming an object by artistic, careful design.[2] God is not a mad scientist, unknowingly experimenting with creation to see what He would come up with. He is a thoughtful, careful, loving, artist who knows exactly what He's after in the process of creation. That means God did not haphazardly create man but was fully aware of His expectations and desires of His creation even before He began.

Genesis 1:26–28 is considered a summary statement of the creation of both men and women. In that summary, though, we find a statement of purpose along with mere description. The key is in the word *image*. Those five letters are jam-packed with fundamental theological truth that gives us insight not only into God's original intent in human creation, but also His ongoing purpose for us in the world. The NET Bible note on the terms *likeness* and *image* is helpful to aid our understanding:

The word *dému* ("likeness") is an abstract noun; its verbal root means "to be like; to resemble." In the Book of Genesis the two terms describe human beings who in some way reflect the form and the function of the creator. The form is more likely stressing the spiritual rather than the physical. The "image of God" would be the God-given mental and spiritual capacities that enable people to **relate to God** and to **serve him by ruling** over the created order as his earthly vice-regents.

In our image, after our likeness. Similar language is used in the instructions for building the tabernacle. Moses was told to make it "according to the pattern" he was shown on the mount (Exod. 25:9–10). Was he shown a form, a replica, of the spiritual sanctuary in the heavenly places? In any case, what was produced on earth functioned as the heavenly sanctuary does, but with limitations.[3]

Man was meant to function like a mirror—something to reflect the image of God into creation. Humanity, made in the image of God, was created to be an earthly representation of who God is. In man's God-given dominion and rule over creation, he was to display the ultimate rule of God in his limited dominion.

Man as an Image Bearer

Representation and Responsibility

As an image bearer, man was to reflect God's heavenly reign on earth. In other words, man represents God by virtue of being in His image. In representing God, man was to glorify the God who created him.

This is an incredible responsibility. Both Genesis 1:28 and 2:15 describe this responsibility as the act of subduing and caring for creation. The general meaning of the verb in those passages appears to be "to bring under one's control for one's advantage." In subduing creation, man is given the ability to use it for his personal benefit on God's terms. In that light, the command in Genesis 1:28 might be paraphrased like this: "Harness its potential and use its resources for your benefit."[4] Since God would later create the woman to come along side the man in this task, it's understood that they together would understand and embrace their role and pass this understanding onto their children.

The word *care* in Genesis 2:15 (NIV) carries a similar sense. The man is called "to work it and keep" (ESV) the garden. In essence, this responsibility was a job. Grudem states,

> Immediately upon creating man in Genesis 2, God puts *man* to work, stewarding and ruling in the world that is *God's* own creation. Man is given responsibility to cultivate the garden, and man is called upon to name the animals. So, while the garden in which man dwells is God's, God gives to man the responsibility to steward it. And, importantly, while the animals are God's, God gives to man the right and responsibility to name them (note especially the statement in Genesis 2:19 that whatever the *man* called the living creature, "that was its name").[5]

Whenever we talk about this at Epiphany Fellowship, the women go crazy. They love hearing that the man got a job before he had a woman! Work was good in those days; more than good, in fact. Then and now, in a redeemed sense, work is a key part of who we are as men.

Man was called to subdue. And he was called to care. But he was also called to rule. In ruling they would serve as God's vice-regents[6] on Earth. This rule was not to be done with an iron fist. If humans were really going to reflect the image of God's rule on their own, they would accept the responsibility of seeing to the welfare of that which is put under them and the privilege of using it for their benefit.[7] Man would have led the effort in that he was the first created and the first to receive these instructions from the Lord (1 Tim. 2:13).

Relationship

We need to be careful here that we don't miss one of the chief components of being God's image bearer. As an image bearer, man is to subdue. He is to care and work. And he is to rule. All these components are key, but what is missing up to this point is the *relationship*. Having a relationship with Yahweh was what made image bearing more than just some sort of political appointment. God designed humans with a unique capacity for relationship because it was His intent that this centerpiece of His creation, man and woman, would be relationally connected to Him for eternity. Without relationship none of the other aspects of being an image bearer would matter. Think about it like this: If a father relates to his children only based on the chores they are supposed to do, that child would grow up with a warped sense of love, accomplishment, and self-worth. Similarly, our relationship with God was intended to be much more than a stale deistic relationship where He creates and leaves things on Earth to us.

Emulsifier chart:

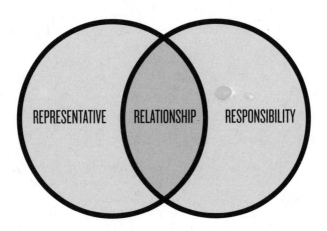

As the chart above points out our identity as God's representatives, our activity of the responsibilities He has given us, and our connectivity to Him in relationship are all aspects of being created in the image of God. However, identity and activity flow from connectivity:

Relationship with God is so central to what it means to be an image bearer that Jeremiah states it is the only thing man can boast about in relation to himself:

> Thus says the LORD: "Let not the wise man boast in his wisdom, let not the mighty man boast in his might, let not the rich man boast in his riches, but let him who boasts boast in this, that he understands and knows me, that I am the LORD who practices steadfast love, justice, and righteousness in the earth. For in these things I delight, declares the LORD." (Jer. 9:23–24 ESV)

The word *know* is a term of intimacy. It's the same word used of God's intimate knowledge of the prophet in Jeremiah 1:5. When God restored man through Jesus Christ, the first thing highlighted isn't ruling or responsibility, but relationship (John 17:3). The point is that relationship is the most compelling factor driving what it means to be made in the image of God.

God gave the first woman to the first man to be a suitable helper to him and to accompany him as a co-image bearer to live out representation, responsibility, and relationship not only in how they related to God but also how they related to each other. The man's form and nature are matched by the woman's as she reflects him and complements him as an equal, yet distinct partner. They correspond to each other. In other words, the woman has everything (in essence and value) that God invested in the man.[8] Therefore, both have an equal relationship with God, but each is distinct in how he or she represents Him and lives out their responsibility toward Him.

What Killed Manhood?

There was much more wrapped up in that piece of fruit in the garden than just a bad decision. With sin, there always is. We talk ourselves into thinking that sin is just a bad choice; it's not. It's much deeper than that for us, just as it was for Adam. When Adam chose willful rebellion against the law of God, he was choosing to forfeit his birthright by rejecting his calling to represent, be responsible, and enjoy his relationship with God, his wife, and the rest of creation. This single act placed in motion the initial and progressive fall of creation and its order, one whose effects still ravage every facet of the world today. We could speak at length on all things that were lost—peace, harmony, joy, order—these were put aside for temporary pleasure.

Did Adam know the full implications of his choice? Probably not. But sin is like that. It blinds us to the consequences of our actions. We get so nearsighted when we see something we want to experience that everything else fades away. Adam chose to set aside his representation of God, responsibility for God, and relationship with God, and these things were lost because of the price of his sin. Although men and women are equal, their function in the fall was different. As the man, Adam is held responsible for it (Rom. 5:12). Sin entered through Adam and spread to men and women alike. When Adam sinned, all of God's intentions for man fell with man. Peace and enjoyment of God and His creation was lost. The spread of God's reign across the earth was lost. Dominion over the world was lost. The development of the undeveloped earth for the Lord was lost. Gone.

Adam made this choice in the most perfect of environments. It would only get worse from there. As more people were born, after the fall in Genesis 3, they would be born without Adam's responsibility, representation, and relationship, at least in the sense that God meant in the beginning. The definition of being an image bearer of God would be marred at the core of man's being for millennia. Man would struggle and replace what was meant to be reflected as a sign of his relationship with Yahweh with himself and creation. Without a relationship with God to navigate and give value to responsibility and relationship, humankind would spiral out of control.

Consequently, manhood was lost along with the rest of God's original design for creation. Instead of responsibility, representation, and relationship, things like chauvinism, violence, passivity, insecurity, and addiction would characterize generation after generation of men in a continually increasing way.

Things Got Worse

Genesis 2:17 records the solemn warning God gave to Adam: he would "surely die," or literally "dying you shall die," if he ate from the tree. The death described ominously here encompasses both a spiritual and physical sense. Physical death is pointing to termination of physical life; worse still, spiritual death means the termination of relationship with God. Once separated from God, men would continue in a downward spiral over the ages as that separation became more and more fully fleshed out.

One of the saddest statements about the state of man is found in Genesis 6:5–6.

> "The LORD saw that the wickedness of man was great in the earth, and that every intention of the thoughts of his heart was only evil continually. And the LORD was sorry that he had made man on the earth, and it grieved him to his heart." (ESV)

Chilling. Man, the centerpiece of God's creative activity, His very representative meant to be the apex of the projection of His glory, was so grievous to God's heart that God was sorry He had ever made man.[9] Since Genesis 3, man continued to devolve until, in Genesis 6, God took an inventory of the state of mankind. All that man intended to be and do was being used for evil intent. Responsibility and representation had fallen to selfish motives of personal gain. Man was using the power that God gave him to rule as a way to dominate and corrupt what God once called good.

Sin Experts

Fast-forward to now, and not much has changed. Things are getting worse, not better. In our cities men are becoming more and more inventive in their acts of crime and violence. If Hollywood is a cultural barometer, which it often is, we can see example after example of our capacity for evil. In the movie *Seven*, two police officers seek to stop a serial killer who justifies his murders by positioning himself as a vigilante creating a murderous masterpiece against those who personified the seven deadly sins: envy, greed, lust, anger, sloth, gluttony, and pride. Each murder is a gory—and creative—depiction of the particular sin of the guilty. The guilty are punished with an even more perverse form of their sin of choice. As you watch the movie, you get a visceral sense at how innovative all of us are at sinning.

The longer creation exists in a state of separation from God, the effects of that separation become more and more clear. First Timothy 3, written thousands of years after the events recorded in Genesis 6, predicts this. And in our world today, two thousand years after Paul penned his letter, the depth of our depravity has come even starker into view. Our separation from God is so embedded that our dysfunction has become the new normal. From music videos to the multibillion-dollar porn industry, you see anywhere and everywhere the effects of the disastrous fall. As Solomon said in Ecclesiastes 8:11, "Because the sentence against an evil deed is not executed speedily, the heart of the children of man is fully set to do evil" (ESV).

Even so, things are not as bad as they could be. God by His grace continues to restrain how comprehensively expressive man's sin is fleshed out in the world. If the Lord gave all of mankind over to the full extent of our sinfulness, we would totally destroy ourselves. In Romans 1:24–28 Paul speaks of God giving already sinful people over to a deeper level of sinfulness. Inferentially, it seems that the Lord somehow restrains this from being a norm in the lives of all fallen humanity. Second Thessalonians 2:7 infers that the Lord in some way holds back the immensity of how destructive evil becomes on the earth. Accordingly, it is only due to the goodness and patience of the living God that any of us are still here, as He has throughout history acted to place a cap on our wickedness.

Throughout the events recorded in the Bible, we see the Lord revealing Himself, disciplining, judging, preaching, performing miracles, and ultimately sending Jesus to keep the clutches of sin from taking full grip on creation. These intervening acts only serve to highlight the full destructive nature of sin:

> As a result of the fall, sin has become universal; except for Jesus Christ no person who ever lived on this earth has been free from sin. This sad fact is acknowledged even by those who are neither adherents of Christianity nor believers of the Bible.[10]

Because the scope of the fall is so great, the solution to the fall must be equally great or greater. Solutions like self-help, community programming, and training groups all have their place, but it's not at the foundation. These can only help to treat the symptoms, to prolong the inevitable. We need something deeper. We need to be born again. Being born again reverses the polarity of creation (John 3). Because sin was the cause, sin must be eradicated for an end to come to the pervasive depravity in the world. And because sin has not only destroyed humanity but creation as well, all of redeemable creation must be re-created—born again in its own way—for things to finally be as they should.

Unfortunately, not all beings in the universe long for this to happen.

Attempts to Assassinate Godly Manhood

From Genesis 3 to the birth of Jesus, Satan has made it his business to destroy any attempts for manhood to be restored. We see his efforts played out in the birth of Adam and Eve's children. Abel was the righteous seed of the woman. His brother, Cain, killed him—the unrighteous seeking to destroy the righteous. The pattern continued in Exodus when Pharaoh commanded that the Hebrew boys be killed in order to lower the number of threats of rebellion, since there were more Hebrews than Egyptians.

Even during the times of captivity of the people of God in the Old Testament, it is believed that Jews who served near the kings were eunuchs. Eunuchs during that time might have held power but weren't considered to be a threat since their peculiar impairment usually rendered them among the most scorned and stigmatized members of society. In a patriarchal culture where honor was tied to male domination, the effeminate, impotent eunuch was viewed with shame and as a threatening social deviant.[11]

Nehemiah, Daniel, Hananiah, Mishael, and Azariah are thought to have been eunuchs. Even with all of the exaltation that they were experiencing in foreign lands, the enemy wanted to make sure that their power was met with shame and limitation of vision. However, even in these times, God gave glimpses of restoration. Each of these men stand the test of time as exemplary, uncompromising men even in the midst of their possible emasculation.

Male genocide and castrating manhood have consistently been the enemy's way to tarnish hope with fear. Keep reading into the New Testament, and you'll see how the knowledge of Jesus' birth drove Herod to strive after the threat to his throne (Matt. 2). All of these physical attempts to bring the end of righteous men only mirror the greater spiritual battle. As men, we must not become lethargic in our vigilance against things that would attempt to destroy manhood.

Literal genocide is no longer politically correct today, but the enemy's threats continue in a more covert form. Homosexuality is of great debate in the world and surprisingly in the church. The redefinition of the family calls for a redefinition of God's intention for the genders. Manhood has to be refined for this ideology to work. This political ideology is a similar tactic to the brutal methods of those biblical rulers. Manhood is under attack. Again. Still. The sooner we realize it's happening, the sooner we can begin to fight back.

CHAPTER 2

The Impact of Daddy Deprivation

 My good friend Blake Wilson, Senior Pastor of Crossover Community Church in Houston, Texas, first coined the phrase "Daddy Deprivation" to describe a trend he was seeing among urban and suburban youth in the church where he worked as a youth pastor. The phrase is a good one—it helps to classify one of the most dangerous and prominent fallen tendencies in our culture when it comes to manhood. Just like Blake, we've seen the same characteristic at play in our church.

Epiphany Fellowship has the great honor of doing ministry in the core of Philadelphia, Pennsylvania. The church serves an incredible variety of people—the indigenous poor, college students, young professionals, a growing seasoned crowd, and artists. The church is ethnically diverse as well, something we have striven for from the very beginning. We initially thought that fatherlessness would be primarily concentrated in the poor ethnic minorities. To our dismay, though, daddy issues have been a cross-ethnic, cross-socioeconomic, cross-generational problem that doesn't discriminate.

A man I will call Nassir lost his father at the tender age of four. All of his life he has struggled with his identity as a man. He admits that being raised in a household mostly of women has been a maturity challenge for him. As he has grown to adulthood, pockets of his memory are lost from between the ages of three and nine. Eventually he became a Christian and the Lord began to aid him in dealing with his past. During that process he realized that he had been molested for a large portion of his childhood. Nassir has come to believe that if his father was still living and a strong presence in his life, the molestations and the subsequent identity crisis of manhood would have been much different.

Rick's father was physically there, but checked out. Though he was present in the home, he was a passive influence on Rick's development into a man and a husband. Because of his father's present absence, Rick resonated greatly with other young men's anger and disdain at their own fathers for physically leaving. He felt bad because at least (in his mind), he knew who his father was. Despite this, he never knew his dad intimately, and consequently didn't know the first thing about being a man.

Then there's Chris. Chris's mom has eight children with three dads between them. The promiscuity she ignored in her youth caught up with her when she was ready to be responsible. Her children wanted to connect with their fathers as they grew older; unfortunately, if she was honest, she wasn't completely clear on the identity of Chris's dad. She assigned fatherhood to the man that she could remember she was sleeping with at the time, but Chris found himself at a loss because he wasn't certain who his father really was.

These are just a few examples of daddy deprivation stories. The epidemic of fatherlessness is one of the most harmful issues in the maturation of men. David Blankenhorn explains:

> A generation ago, an American child could reasonably expect to grow up with his father. Today, an American child can reasonably expect not to. Fatherlessness is now approaching a rough parity with fatherhood as a defining feature of American childhood.
>
> The astonishing fact is reflected in many statistics, but here are the two most important. Tonight, about 40 percent of American children will go to sleep in homes in which their fathers do not live. Before they reach the age of eighteen, more than half of our nation's children are likely to spend at least a significant portion of their childhoods living apart from their fathers. Never before in this country have so many children been voluntarily abandoned by their father. Never before have so many children grown up without knowing what it means to have a father.
>
> Fatherlessness is the most harmful demographic trend of this generation. It is the leading cause of declining child well-being in our society. It is also the engine driving our most urgent social problems, from crime to adolescent pregnancy to child sexual abuse to domestic violence against women. Yet, despite its scale

and social consequences, fatherlessness is a problem that is frequently ignored or denied. Especially within our elite discourse, it remains largely a problem with no name.[1]

His book, *Fatherless America*, was published in the mid-1990s. The trend that was devastating then has increased beyond measure. Among the more devastating effects of daddy deprivation on boys is an ongoing sense of identity crisis. Without fathers, young boys have no sense of who they are and who they are called to be as men. It only makes sense that it would be this way, given that a boy's earthly father is suppose to establish this clarity of identity early in life.

The result is a tremendous loss of self. So acute is this brokenness that men have become incredibly adept at diverting our focus from what is missing. We develop habits, judge one another's manhood, and turn to various abuses all to cover up what is really missing—our fathers. In the end, though, despite these attempts to cover up what's missing, a man will find something to use as a replacement or surrogate for their father.

Daddy Replacements

God was intentional in His original design of the human body, emotions, and development. Everything He originally designed to be in our lives was essential. When some key piece of what He designed is missing, man will search for a replacement. Though not all replacements are bad, most of the time we err on the side of our fallenness.

We are the same way as humans. Many times we don't recognize what God has given us and we are willing to trade it for something else that looks decent but can't compare to what He has already provided. Anything we try and use as a replacement for God's original intention is dysfunctional in some way and only causes more ruin. Mankind has always been in the business of giving away the greatness of what God has provided for that which is substandard (Jer. 2:11–13; Rom. 1:21–23).

Artists

Identity has become an artistic creation of man's choosing. In this line of thinking, who you are is based on personal wish and desire as opposed to being rooted in the image of God. This is particularly visible in the hip-hop world, one of pop culture's greatest global missionaries. From plastic surgery, body tattoos, fashion, what crew someone is apart of or trying to create, artist branding is synonymous with identity.

In this soup of creativity, manhood is relative. Even more startling is how many artists utilize their lack of natural fathering and their survival through it as kind of the rite of passage to success. 50 Cent was asked in an interview, "Would you be the same artist if your father was active in your life?" He emphatically stated, "No!"—letting the interviewer know that having a father would have removed all of the content of what he has become popular for. The interviewer continued, "Do you wanna know who your father is now?" His response echoes the sentiment of many: "No! What is the use now?" But there is another undercurrent that is taking shape.

Lil Wayne and Bryan "Baby" Williams have had a long-standing relationship as father and son. In many ways their relationship has personified for a generation what a father really is—the cool father is down for you no matter what. At one point a few years back, the two even shared a kiss in the mouth. Despite the allegations of homosexuality leveled at them, they responded less with a defense of their actions and more of an affirmation of the type of connection they share as father and son. So while 50 Cent has no interest in fatherhood, there is a latent longing expressed in others. It's a longing for the lost connection.

Gay Parents

As of late, the issue of parenting has been expanded. In the past, the lack of true fatherhood was mainly discussed surrounding single-parent homes and divorce. But with the rise of lesbian, gay, bisexual, and transgender parenting (LGBT), a broader crisis in parenting and fatherhood. In years past, this community desired an acknowledgment of their validity through legitimizing their relationships. But the effort is underway to expand this understanding so that a "family" can be redefined any way the particular members want it to be. It's another step toward culturally normalizing LGBT as a part of humanities options. A magazine promoting this philosophy in the tri-state area reads as follows:

> Thinking of becoming a parent? Looking to expand your family through foster care, adoption or reproductive technology? Want to find an LGBT friendly private school or camp for your child? How did other

LGBTs become parents or deal with issues with their child? *Gay Parent* magazine (GPM) can help you answer questions about same sex and gay parenting.

GPM is a 16 to 48 page bound newsprint magazine featuring personal stories of LGBT parents from across the country and around the world—we take you into their homes. Parents speak candidly about their experiences with international and domestic adoption, foster care, donor insemination, using a surrogate, parenting with an ex, coming out after being in a straight marriage and what it is like to raise their children in their part of the world.[2]

LGBT is more than just a sexual issue, but it rails against gender clarity that facilitates men walking in their divine orientation according to God's created order. God's love for LGBT is just as unconditional, everlasting, and can be remedied through the transformational power of the gospel (1 Cor. 6:9–12). However, the effects of these changes in the family will be seen in the years to come. From a biblical standpoint, this effort isn't normalization; it's genocide of the family, procreation, and gender. As the LGBT community stretches into this final frontier, it will push fatherhood to borders of disintegration.

Single Mothers

Single-parent homes are probably the most challenging dysfunction plaguing the development of men. The Census Bureau's 1997 report has staggering numbers.

Profile of Children's Living Arrangements
(Children Under Age 18)[3]

- In 1995, 48.3 million of the 70.3 million children under age 18 lived with two parents (69 percent); 18.9 million lived with only one parent (27 percent); and 3.0 million lived with neither parent (4 percent).

- Of children living with one parent, 38 percent lived with a divorced parent, 35 percent with a never married parent, 19 percent with a separated parent, 4 percent with a widowed parent, and 4 percent with a parent whose spouse lived elsewhere because of business or some other reason.

- Four million children lived in the homes of their grandparents; for 11 percent of them, both parents were also in the household; for 52 percent, one parent was there; and for 37 percent, neither parent was present.

- Most single parent children live in metropolitan areas (14.5 million), and six in 10 of them (9.2 million) are in cities with populations of 1 million or more.

Thugs

In inner-city communities, fatherlessness is heightened for a number of reasons including crime, cultural socialization, economic depression, the ratio of men to women, and imprisonment. Philadelphia, for example, is estimated to consist of 90 percent single-parent homes.

Mothers in Section 8 projects and rental properties fight to raise their children to live beyond the context of their community. But even if they escape, the father wounds plague the psyche of boys trying to make sense of themselves in a locale where survival is paramount. The images of manhood are limited to the TV and the neighborhood, both of which tend to portray manhood as thuggish. In these neighborhoods, thugs are looked up to for their knack of being able to navigate the harsh terrain of the hood. Observing this, boys desire that same level of prowess. Thugs, then, become viable candidates for the predominant image of manhood.

In their own way, each of these situations is an effort to fill the void left by absent fathers. And in each case, the replacement falls dramatically short of what God originally intended. It's to this original intent we turn next.

God's Intention for Fatherhood

God's design has always been that men would be fathered. That earthly fathers would be a representation of a heavenly One. Somehow Adam understood this when he gave his prophetic utterance about his union with Eve, "This is why a man leaves his father and mother and bonds with his wife, and they become one flesh" (Gen. 2:24). Several basic observations can be made from this Scripture.

1. The fact that man has to leave his parents and bond to his wife assumes a parental bond.
2. Fatherhood is assumed in God's design.
3. The presence and impact of a father is an essential part of that design.

For the first time in Scripture the word *father* is used. These implications will be passed along throughout the Bible.

Father as Clarifier of Identity

Along with the rest of the Old Testament, Genesis frames fatherhood as an essential part of cultic life. The identity of sons as well as entire households and clans were deeply connected to the identity of a father figure. God Himself employs similar language in how He reveals Himself to people in the patriarchal period:

> And behold, the LORD stood above it and said, "I am the LORD, the God of Abraham *your father* and the God of Isaac. (Gen. 28:13 ESV)

In that time, the absence of fathers would have thrown society fully out of social, economic, spiritual, and geographical balance:

> In the patriarchal worldview of biblical Israel, the father was the linchpin of family life, and his house was the basic unit of biblical society. Fatherhood was the only way a man could perpetuate his name and memory after death. Thus the acquisition of male heirs is often a primary element in biblical narratives. (e.g., 1 Sam. 1)[4]

One of the most powerful passages illustrative of the link between the identity of sons and their fathers is found in Genesis 49. In this chapter, Jacob calls his sons to him. He then proceeds to speak into the lives of those young men, helping them understand their true identity just as his own father, Isaac, had done for him (even though Isaac's actions were under deception). Such a charge would have secured his sons in who they were; it was a way of establishing their identity and charging them with responsibility.

Verse 28 marks the conclusion of this blessing: "These are the tribes of Israel, 12 in all, and this was what their father said to them. He blessed them, and he blessed each one with a suitable blessing." Literally, the Hebrew here is "and he blessed them, each of whom according to his blessing, he blessed them."[5] In other words, the blessing properly matched the son. Although Jacob's sons had issues, Daddy did his job in the midst of this blended and dysfunctional family.

The Father as Spiritual Leader

At the center of the father's responsibility was the spiritual leadership that he exercised under the headship of Yahweh. This leadership would permeate every single area of the family's life and function. Though fathers were to execute this role in partnership with the mother, the primary responsibility fell to the dad. The proverbs, for example, make frequent use of the term "my son" intrinsically connecting with discipleship.[6] In his writing of Proverbs 1, Solomon spoke of his role in the life of his son as an instructor—trainer as well as disciplinarian. One commentator describes the father's role as discipler in the household like this:

A father's central religious duty was to see that his son was circumcised into the covenant (Lev. 12:3) and instructed properly in the Lord's torah (Deut. 11:19).

In the book of Proverbs, the father provides proper instruction about living well and responsibly within society for his sons. In biblical narratives sons leave their fathers' house to follow divine command (Gen. 12:1) or to escape criminal punishment (27:41–45; 2 Sam. 13:34–38). More often a father arranged endogamous marriages for his sons and welcomed his daughters-in-law into his home (Gen. 12:2–6; but cf. Cant. 4:9–10; 5:1–2). In addition, the father was responsible for supervising the behavior (Num. 12:14) and the sexuality of the women who lived within his house; in this way, he guaranteed that children born to his wife were his and that his daughters were virgins when they left his house for marriage. He exercised absolute authority over his children, but especially over his daughters, whose status within the household was inferior and precarious (2 Sam. 13). They returned to his control if they were widowed without children. If their behavior shamed him, they deserved death (Gen. 38:24; cf. Judg. 11:35–36).[7]

True, some of this concept was unique to that culture. Nevertheless, it's clear that such standards would still be of great help—a kind of primer or standard of what is expected. As it is, though, young men are forced to wing it when it comes to manhood. This lack of clear expectations and standards has contributed to the crime rate, unemployment, depression, sexual confusion, and family decay. But if we are to have a return to some kind of cultural standard for fatherhood, it can only come through God, expressed through His people.

God as Father

God the Father is co-equal leader of the Godhead (Ps. 110:1). Throughout the Bible He is lifted up as Father, emphasizing (as Jesus did in the Lord's Prayer), His desire for intimacy and covenant connection.

God the Spirit Reveals God as Father

So central is God's role as Father those transformed through the gospel of Jesus Christ that one of the roles of the Holy Spirit is to make sure believers know God as Father (Rom. 8:15–16). The Holy Spirit encourages us to relate to God as Father. He causes us to call Him "Abba." Abba is a term of intimacy that children had with their father:

> The idea of God's intimate relationship to humanity is a distinct feature of Jesus' teaching. God relates to believers as a father relates to his child. Some would translate *Abba* as "Daddy" to convey the close, personal meaning of the word. Even when "Father" in the NT translates the more formal Greek word *pater*, the idea of *Abba* is certainly in the background. Jesus addressed God as *Abba* in prayer (Mark 14:36) and taught His disciples to pray in the same terms (Luke 11:1–2, *pater*). Jesus' claim of intimate relationship with God offended many of His opponents because they considered *Abba* to be overly familiar in addressing God. Nevertheless, Jesus' usage established the

pattern for the church's view of God and each believer's relationship with Him.[8]

Students of the New Testament have rightly called the Holy Spirit the "Spirit of Adoption." Being the Spirit of Adoption, one of the roles of the Spirit is to affirm in the soul of the believer that they are partakers of the inheritance[9] of God the Father through belief in Jesus. Inheritance was a deep part of a son's connection and relationship to his father. The knowledge of a sure and certain inheritance provides a son with a deep sense of connectedness to who he is. This is what the Holy Spirit does for the believer; He reminds us of our irrevocable spiritual inheritance of God—on the full restoration of our souls and bodies in eternity with our Father (2 Cor. 5:1–5). The Spirit can guarantee this because He assures us that God the Father is not a deadbeat dad, but a responsible and present one. By the presence of the Spirit in our lives, He has sealed us to preserve us for our Father (Eph. 1:14).

Romans 8 points to a similar truth. The context of this passage was one of crisis where believers weren't so much struggling with their identity but their very existence in a fallen world. The persecutions and temptations of the world are a constant reminder that we cannot yet enjoy full fellowship with our Father, so the Spirit aids us in our groanings to be revealed fully as children of God. Even creation wants this (Rom. 8:18–23). Armed with the Spirit, reminding us of the fatherhood of God, the Christian can live in confident obedience to the call, command, and responsibility before him.

God the Son Reveals God as Father

Although His ministry was to show a comprehensive view of who God is, no other human explained God the Father more effectively than Jesus. God's fatherhood of us is rooted in God's fatherhood of Jesus. Jesus' entire earthly ministry was driven by His understanding of and His relationship with God as His Father (John 1:18). The Son has been in eternal fellowship with the Father. Jesus' identity and mission as God the Son was understood and lived out in light of the Father's love for Him (John 5:19–20). In essence, Jesus knew His Father, spent time with His Father, and knew that His Father loved Him. He could even suffer a brutal death because of His knowledge of the pleasure the Father would express because of His death (Isa. 53:10). He was, through His life, revealing what He had experienced of God as His Father to the rest of humanity.

Because Jesus knew God as His Father, He knew exactly what His life and mission were about. Conversely, without the Fatherhood of God driving our manhood, we become "mad scientists" as we destructively experiment with those in our charge.[10] But because of Jesus, there is hope.

Even in the absence of earthly fathers, the gospel's impact and the Spirit's presence is sufficient to guide us through the pool of daddy deprivation. The fatherless man can find strength in the fatherhood of God. Through a relationship with the Lord Jesus Christ, God becomes our Father. He is proud of His children because He is pleased with His Son who lives in them. In Jesus, God was and is calling those who are

His children as they hear His voice and respond by the power of the Holy Spirit (John 8:39–47; 10:22–30).

Extended Adolescence and Biblical Maturity

My undergraduate degree was in psychology. As I began to study human development, we discussed the stage of development called "adolescence." Initially, adolescence was understood to begin at puberty and end either in the early twenties, late teens, or when one sensed some level of independence. This stage was seen as the incubator of pre-adulthood.

In my classes, we agreed that boys go through seminal emissions, facial hair growth, deepening of the voice, muscular development, heightened sexual desire, and identity curiosity. But the class had a heated discussion on what marked the transition out of this stage. Looking back, we focused so much on adolescence, that we never discovered how we would define manhood and womanhood. As the class continued, everyone (no matter the worldview) came to the conclusion that this stage in human development was a Western invention that postponed the responsibility of adulthood to a later date. From a general revelation standpoint, everyone agreed that there is only childhood and adulthood. Irresponsibility and responsibility. Immaturity and maturity.

That was years ago. But what we're finding now, both through study and mere observation, is that "childhood" is growing longer and longer. Boys are not only failing to become responsible and godly men; they aren't becoming men at all. The problems with this extended childhood are many:

1. *Compromised maturity.* Men may have adult bodies, but they remain spiritual infants.

2. *Fathers who are only friends.* Men in extended childhood seek to identify with their children as opposed to raise their children. Their efforts at parenting are like their efforts in high school—to be liked and accepted rather than to influence and guide.

3. *Subsidized pictorial of manhood.* When a younger male sees a man living like this, the problem is heightened because extended childhood becomes the picture of what a man should be.

4. *Unmarried women.* As the pool of men is already quite slim for women, it will get even more challenging as they are faced with men who are unfit for marriage.

5. *Un-hirable men.* Men in this stage can work at a job that requires physical maturity but will be incapable of functioning in a professional environment that demands maturity and responsibility.

6. *Life lived in fantasy.* This might be most frightening of all. Men in extended childhood treat their lives like one, big fantasy world. They engage others through artificial means like pornography, social media, and video games instead of real life. In their fantasy world, everything revolves around them, so they are incapable of contributing to a family, church, or community because all of them require sacrifice.

Emotional Immaturity

In his landmark book *Emotionally Healthy Spirituality*, Peter Scazzero lays out a basic description of what it looks like to be emotionally healthy and unhealthy. One of the most striking points of this work is his description of emotional immaturity:

Emotional Infants[11]

- Look for others to take care of them
- Have great difficulty entering into the world of others
- Are driven by need for instant gratification
- Use others as objects to meet their needs

Emotional Children[12]

- Are content and happy as long as they receive what they want
- Unravel quickly from stress, disappointments, trials
- Interpret disagreements as personal offenses
- Are easily hurt
- Complain, withdraw, manipulate, take revenge, become sarcastic when they don't get their way
- Have great difficulty calmly discussing their needs and wants in a mature, loving way

Sound familiar? Most men wouldn't own up to this kind of description, but mere observation validates the finding above. One of the root causes of prolonged childhood in adulthood is the lack of emotional growth. According to Scazzero emotional immaturity many times stems from ignoring the past's impact on the present. When this happens, in my estimation, we place ourselves in a state of stasis that doesn't allow us to grow emotionally beyond whatever trauma or disappointment that holds us in bondage.

In a Bible study we did for the men at Epiphany Fellowship on the life of Jacob from the book of Genesis, we saw how God forced Jacob to overcome the impact of his past on his present and his future. The outline of that study, which we called "Dealing with Your Past," provides an introduction as to how God moves men through confronting what has stunted their growth and then pass it:

- An incident (Gen. 25:29–34; 27)
- Pending consequences and pain (Gen. 27:41)
- Runs from his problems (Gen. 27:42–28:10)
- God gives him promises for his journey (Gen. 28:10–15)
- Jacob acknowledges God's presence (Gen. 28:16–22)
- Tries to secure the blessings of God with human effort

    - Lies (Gen. 25:29–34)
    - Deceit (Gen. 27:1–30)
    - Experiencing the reaping of what he has sown (Gen. 29:15–30)

- God teaches Jacob

    - How to respond to His voice (Gen. 31:3)
    - Recognition of God's continued presence (Gen. 31:5)
    - Recognition of God's protection (Gen. 31:6)
    - How to deal with conflict (Gen. 31:33–55)

- God placed Him alone (Gen. 32:24)
- God forces Jacob out of his wits to dependence by breaking him (Gen. 32:24–32)
- Jacob faces his past on God's terms (Gen. 34)

God's View of Manhood Development

We see a similar pattern in 1 Corinthians 13, a statement from Paul that even many non-Christians will quote as a maxim for development: "When I was a child, I spoke like a child, I thought like a child, I reasoned like a child. When I became a man, I gave up childish ways" (1 Cor. 13:11 ESV). Although in context, this verse is about spiritual maturity in the use of spiritual gifts, you can see the pattern of overall development into maturity at play. It's interesting that the Bible doesn't particularly identify the transition from childhood to manhood as a mere transition of physical development as we typically do in Western culture. But the Western definition of adolescence, as we'll soon see, does align remarkably well with the biblical definition of childhood.

The Bible contains descriptions of transitions of men into maturity that serve as a good gauge of how men develop. In its pages we find references to childhood, youth, young men, and old men, each with its own characteristics, traits, and associated responsibilities. The book of Proverbs gives us insight into the heart of a child. If you look closely, you'll see confirmation of the fact that many men in Western culture, though physically mature, still exist in this state.

Proverbs 22:15 describes children this way. "Folly is bound up in the heart of a child, but the rod of discipline drives it

far from him" (ESV). The description is enlightening. The NET
Bible states, "The "heart of a child" refers here to the natural
inclination of a child to foolishness. Though this verse primarily refers to a child young in age, the word can include youth.
R. N. Whybray suggests that this idea might be described
as a doctrine of "original folly." The Good News Translation
expounds on the idea, saying that "children just naturally do
silly, careless things." It describes ages from birth through
teenage years (Gen. 37:2). In this passage discipline and training is the way to help prepare the child for manhood.

The word *folly* brings clarity regarding the maturity level
of the child at this point in their life. "Folly" is a state of being
devoid of wisdom and understanding, with a focus on the evil
behaviors, which occur in this state.[13] "Bound up" points to
foolishness being tied to the heart of the child. This is remarkably similar to the description in our culture of adolescence.
The emphasis in the passage is on preparation—the stage in
which boys are rightly and fully prepared for adulthood.

CHAPTER 3

The Restorer of Manhood

 All right, I'll admit it: I watch the Food Network. And HGTV. And DIY. One by one, my wife has gotten me sucked into all these channels, especially the shows that deal with the restoration of homes. I remember one show in particular when a couple bought a house "as is" and were excited about the challenge of transforming what "as is" into what "could be." Upon inspection, however, they found all sorts of issues: Structural issues, asbestos, and black mold all had to be addressed. These were deeper issues than the kind of flowers planted in the beds out front or the color the shutters were to be painted. But the couple realized that though fixing these things was behind-the-scenes kind of work, they were fundamental and core to the restoration. Only if they addressed the deeper issues in the home, would they be able to truly enjoy the full restoration in the long-term.

Jesus, as God's general contractor, is looking at our lives and making the same claim. There are some things deeply and fundamentally wrong with us. But fortunately, He has not come to bring mere aesthetic changes, but systemic restoration. For although He will change the way the world looks (Rev. 21), He will first transform the core of what messed the world up in the first place. In transforming the soul of sinful man, Jesus will set in motion an eternal chain reaction that will change all things forever (1 Cor. 15).

Jesus the Restorer of All Things

Jesus is the means by which everything will be restored. Though the Bible has much to say about the subject of restoration, most of the uses of this word are connected to Jesus in both the Old Testament and New. Because of Adam's sin, Jesus will restore all things for the Father.

Restoration is the act of returning something to its original state. The Bible has a slightly different take on the word, because sometimes when it speaks of restoration, it is not returning something to an original state, but to a state it has not been in before. In either case, though, restoration is about being in an originally intended state—it's about God's holy intention for it. In the Old Testament, we find many references to restoration concerning the work of God to bring about His intentions for something based on a promise, trajectory, or reality with those in covenant with Him. The people of Judah, for example, eventually went into captivity. But before they did, the Lord promised them that He would restore them to His original intentions for them (Jer. 29:14). Restoration, then, is about God's people experiencing the fullness of His promises by His grace. Only one problem—this restoration never happened because the people of God were unable to walk in such a way before God that they could experience the fullness of God's promise. Over and over again Yahweh gave the people of God chances to be restored to Him, and over and over again they chose sin instead.

Haggai 2:9 shows us something similar. God promised that the glory of the second temple would be greater than the former, but because of the people's failure to walk purely before Him, the glory didn't return in stunning fashion. The second temple paled in comparison to the first, despite God's desire for restoration. Again, sin tarnished the extent of restoration. God's people needed help if they were going to experience the fullness of His restorative promises. The Messiah is promised in Isaiah 54 to be the restorer of all things. Upon His arrival, this Messiah would set in order all things based on the eternal intentions of Yahweh.

Jesus Has Restored All Things

It is impossible to talk about restoration without talking about reconciliation. *Reconciliation* is a term that assumes discord in relationships, a discord initiated by an act of offense by at least one party in the relationship. Colossians 1:20 is the staple passage concerning reconciliation in Christ, one that reveals the source of the discord as well as the source of the solution:

The word there used refers to a change wrought in the personal character of the sinner who ceases to be an enemy to God by wicked works, and yields up to him his full confidence and love. In 2 Cor. 5:20 the apostle beseeches the Corinthians to be "reconciled to God," i.e., to lay aside their enmity.[1]

In a sense, this restoration is already fully accomplished by Jesus. The cross makes it a done deal. Through the cross, we have been fully reconciled to God in Christ, and our restoration is therefore a present reality: "For if, while we were enemies, we were reconciled to God through the death of His Son, then how much more, having been reconciled, will we be saved by His life!" (Rom. 5:10). The greatness of the cross cannot be overstated. Through His death and resurrection, Jesus has restored all things. And yet this restoration is not yet fully realized. So Jesus is also restoring all things.

Jesus Is Restoring All Things

The restoration of Jesus is fully accomplished but not fully realized. It is "already, but not yet." In this interim time, between the ascension and second coming of Jesus, there is work to be done, and Jesus uses us as His agents of reconciliation and restoration. In 2 Corinthians 5:20, Paul pictured Christians as ambassadors of reconciliation and restoration. As ambassadors, we are His representatives on earth who participate in His work of restoring all things to Himself (Titus 2:11–15).

Jesus Will Restore All Things

Jesus has restored all things. Jesus is restoring all things. And gloriously, we are confident that Jesus *will* restore all things. Someday, we will have the beautiful honor of experiencing the full transformation of all creation (Rev. 21). One day the heavens and the earth will pass away and all things will be fully new to be enjoyed with God being all and in all. His reign will be indiscriminately revealed for all to see. Let's look a little deeper at Jesus in order to see just how this restoration has happened, is happening, and eventually will happen.

Jesus, the Prototype Man

I used to collect vintage action figures. DC, Marvel, G.I. Joe, Masters of the Universe—I had them all. As I got deeper into collecting, I discovered that as part of the manufacturing process these companies typically created a prototype of the action figures prior to creating the others. This prototype acted as the mold or standard by which those coming after it would be created and judged. Because it was the first, and therefore set the standard for the others, the prototype over time became recognized as the most valuable because from it all others were made.

Jesus is the prototype man for men. All of us men are only as manly as it relates to the standard set by Jesus. Romans 8:29 helps us to understand this point: "For those He foreknew He also predestined to be conformed to the image of His Son, so that He would be the firstborn among many brothers." God's design—His divine intent—is for those who are in Jesus to look like Jesus.

God predestined his people *to be conformed to the likeness of his Son.* We are to become like Christ (cf. 1 John 3:1), which, as Hendriksen points out, means sanctification. It is God's plan that his people become like his Son, not that they should muddle along in a modest respectability. We should be in no doubt as to the high standard that Paul sets for Christian people. We have been admitted to the heavenly family; we are *brothers* in that family and we call God "Father." We are accordingly to live as members of the family, and that means being made like our elder Brother. This is all part of God's predestination; he predestined us not only to be released from an unpleasant predicament, but in order that we might become like his Son.[2]

This is an incredibly high calling. Trace it back with me: It's God's intention that we become like Jesus. And Jesus is the image of the invisible God (Col. 1:15). You start to see, yet again, the greatness of God's original intent for humanity. Jesus, then, is the true prototype man—the second Adam—coming to restore men to the image that was lost through the first Adam.

I once knew a phenomenal artist whose medium was sculpture. I was fascinated when I watched him work—by the hand control and skill it took to chisel stone into a smooth and clear image. I asked him once about his technique, and his response has stuck with me: "When you look at this stone you see a rock, but when I look at it I see an image in the rock. All I am trying to do is get to the image by removing everything else in the way." That is what God does through the process of restoration. We have been restored already, and yet we are still being restored. The image is there, but a lot is left around it. Sanctification, then, is God's work, through the Holy Spirit, to chisel us into the image He sees in us. This isn't so much a physical conformity (although we will be "like" Jesus in our new glorified bodies); rather, this is soul work. Furthermore, it is the work, particularly in men, that has been neglected.

Growing up in a city that was riddled with violence, crime, and fatherlessness, there were very few images of manhood that reflected the Lord Jesus Christ. Even when I went into the church, the paintings of Jesus I saw showed a soft-skinned man with long flowing hair whose clothes were always clean. That didn't really connect with a young man like me, growing up in the Black-Power/hip-hop era.

More and more, I found myself being influenced in those days by Black Nationalistic rhetoric from sources like Malcolm X, Farrakhan, and Elijah Mohammad. They presented something different from those pictures at the church. I saw in them a form of disciplined manliness. They even presented Jesus as a masculine black man with some fight in Him. They railed against the white and feminized images of Jesus in the American church. Their understanding of Jesus might have been ethnocentric, but there was something appealing about it nonetheless. Now, looking back, I think what I finally saw was Jesus as a man—real man. And that was something new for me.

Years later, the church is still primarily built on engaging issues that are more pertinent to women. Somewhere along the line, we recognized in the church—either consciously or subconsciously—that men are often harder to reach, and we didn't put forth the time or effort to do so. As a consequence, more and more men began to see church as a place for the women. Like it or not, men view the church as irrelevant because much of what concerns men is either not addressed or when it is talked about it is done so in a feminine manner. Dr. Carl Ellis writes,

> Core concerns come in three categories: *personal, social,* and *cultural. Personal core concerns* include things like loneliness, anxiety, and fear. These tend to be unchanging and universal. *Social core concerns* include things like education, health, and family. *Cultural core concerns* are directly related to particular situations and tend to be unique to each people group.[3]

It's important to understand this because it holds the key on how to most effectively communicate to men. As Ellis says, you can't communicate with men at a core level by going straight to personal concerns. Rather, it's much more effective to address cultural concerns, then social concerns, then personal concerns. In other words when we deal with the outer rim issues in the life of men we get to the inner life of men. If you compare that to the way that most churches operate, you see that we simply aren't set up to reach men. But Jesus was.

Jesus was able to engage men at all these levels. He dealt with cultural concerns by engaging issues related to the nation (John 8; 10). He dealt with social concerns through healing and teaching on the family (Matt. 8; 19). Jesus also got down to very personal issues with men (John 3). He was, and is, able to engage men on every issue and every level.

Perhaps, then, men are so unclear about who they are supposed to be because we in the church have failed to give them a true picture of the ultimate man Jesus Christ. This man alone was unflawed and untouched by the destructive properties of sin. Yet this man was still born with all of the limitations and temptations of humanity (Heb. 4:15). Jesus, and Jesus alone, has exemplified manhood. If we want to be conformed to His image, most especially as men, we need to understand this example more deeply.

Jesus the Incarnate God-Man

God became man. They are only three words, yet entire volumes have been written on the subject. Despite all that writing, we still fall short in our understanding of exactly how this happened. Nevertheless, the incarnation stands at the core of redemption as a whole, and maybe even particularly so for men.

Jesus, who was and is and will ever be God, also took on flesh. In this taking on, however, He did not sacrifice His divinity. In Christ, then, we find One who is both fully God and fully man: "who, existing in the form of God, did not consider equality with God as something to be used for His own advantage. Instead He emptied Himself by assuming the form of a slave, taking on the likeness of men" (Phil. 2:6–7).

Notice the language in this bedrock passage. Jesus "existed" as God, yet took on the "form" of a man, even a slave. Somehow, a human nature was added to Him without compromising either one. Therefore He has both a divine nature and a sinless human nature without the mixture of the two, yet He is one person. This is key to understanding the greatness of Jesus, because it reminds us that Jesus didn't cheat. He was fully human and was faced with the same temptations common to all of us. Jesus, and Jesus alone, stands apart as the perfect man, for not only was He born that way—perfectly God but also perfectly man—He remained perfect in His humanity. The Westminster Catechism VIII. II states it like this: "two whole, perfect, and distinct natures, the Godhead and the Manhood, were inseparably joined together in one person, without conversion, composition, or confusion."

Son of Man

Jesus often identified Himself as the "Son of Man." This is language lifted straight from the Old Testament. In Daniel 7:13, for example, the term describes a divine man, a passage Jesus quotes about Himself in Luke 21:27. His reference there indicates that He is more than just a man; He is One who has existed eternally. This correlates with another title used in Daniel 7—that of the Ancient of Days. The Son of Man, then, is older than time itself.

This wasn't the only time Jesus referenced this passage in Daniel:

> There are three references to a future coming of the Son of man "in clouds with great power and glory" to gather his chosen people and reject (literally "be ashamed of") those who were ashamed of Jesus (*see*

Apocalyptic Teaching); this coming is associated with his being seated on the right hand of God (Mark 8:38; 13:26; 14:62). Mark 13:26 and 14:62 are clearly reminiscent of Daniel 7:13–14 where a figure "like a son of man" comes with the clouds of heaven, appears before God and is given everlasting sovereign power and dominion (see Kingdom of God).[4]

Jesus will be eternally a man and still eternally God. This exalted man will rule over all creation seen and unseen. The redeemed will worship and adore Him for all eternity. As the "Son of Man," Jesus is describing Himself as without beginning or end; He is divine in connection with Daniel's statements concerning His identity.

But on the other hand, the title also emphasizes His authority as the ultimate human who, despite His greatness, is amazingly humble (Luke 9:58). This is one of the primary qualities of the character of Jesus. His humility, as the Son of Man, is what in fact enables Him to face the death destined for Him:

Jesus speaks of the impending suffering, death and resurrection of the Son of man in a series of predictions which emphasize that this must happen in accordance with the Scriptures; he speaks of the mission of the Son of man as being to serve others and to give his life as a ransom for many, and he speaks of himself as the Son of man in references to his impending betrayal and arrest (Mark 8:31; 9:9, 12, 31; 10:33, 45; 14:21, 41; *see* Predictions of Jesus' Passion and

Resurrection). The threefold repetition of the prediction in Mark is particularly impressive. The sufferings of Jesus are clearly linked to his role as the Son of man; they are not mentioned explicitly without some reference to him as the Son of man.[5]

As the Son of Man, Jesus can relate to any man who has been betrayed, to anyone who has been handed over or mistreated. The difference between most men and Jesus is that when such things happened to Jesus, He dealt with the situation with great righteousness and patience. This was not a sign of weakness; it was a sign of true strength. Only a man of great strength could courageously take that kind of punishment and not cry out that their rights had been violated. Only a man of true strength could endure the cross and all it held without casting the blame on someone else.

Jesus, as the Son of Man, is not only inspirational—He is epic.

Knowing that He got up from the grave after such a savage and brutal martyrdom should make us as men pump our fists in the air in worship. Here before us is a man who was man enough to drink in death and spit out victory. He is fully God and yet truly and fully human. He is a man just like—and yet wholly unlike—us, all at the same time. So if we're looking for an example of manhood, we need look no further than the cross and the empty tomb. Jesus, over and over again, shows us what it means to really be a man.

His Commitment to Facing Sin Head-on (Gen. 3)

One of the ways we see Jesus living as the prototypical man is in His willingness to do something typically very difficult for us—confront sin head-on. Doing so is difficult because it always involves conflict, one in which a wrongdoer is called out and confronted. Jesus doesn't shy away from that kind of confrontation. When we talk about facing sin head-on, no one has been, is, or will ever be as skilled and up front as Jesus Christ.

Think about it—the very fact that Jesus came to Earth is evidence of His willingness to stare sin in the eye. In Jesus Christ, God became human. He chose to live in the world that man had destroyed. He faced fatigue, sweat, hunger, and even rejection. He faced the self-righteous sin of religious people. He faced the self-preserving sin of His closest friends who abandoned Him. He faced being misunderstood by His family, mocked by society, maligned by the crowds, and even stolen from by the soldiers. That's just a small sampling of the rest of the sin that He took upon His shoulders at the cross. And yet He went on.

This is manliness at its best. It's courage at its greatest. It's self-sacrifice at its most noble. It's the fight at its most tenacious. And as a result, man is restored both to potentially be what God originally intended, but then also to enjoy the fullness of fellowship with God that was lost.

Part of that fullness is the restoration of the created order. God had a definite design for the order of creation. Under Himself would be man, woman, and then animals. Simple enough, right? But Satan attempted to distort God's order of creation. He presented it as animals (in his appearance as the snake), woman (through his temptation of the woman rather than the man), and then finally the man.

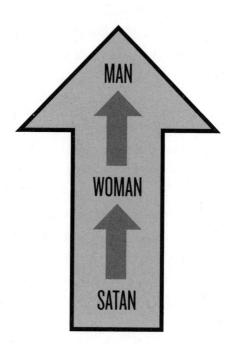

Much of the world lives according to this distorted order. We worship the creation rather than the Creator, and women are the spiritual leaders in the home (if there is one at all). But Jesus is bringing a restored order to things. He's putting things back the way they always should have been.

Restored Order (I Cor. 11:2)

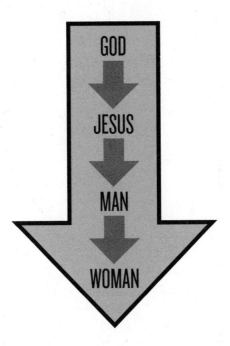

Through Christ, the order, roles, and functions of all creation can find their true intent. Because a relationship with the living God is restored, the relationship between man and woman can also be restored. In this, man brings glory to the new Adam instead of being under the curse of the first one.

Jesus is the paradigm for the new man. Through His courage to face sin, His restoration of order, and His status as the Son of Man, He not only serves as our example; He is the means by which any of us can really understand and be what God intended a man to be. Let's take a look at some of these characteristics the Son of Man displays and then equips men to live with.

The Driven Jesus

In hip-hop culture, there is a concept that has influenced pop culture called *grind*. The "grind" is a multifaceted work ethic driven by a passion to impact culture, make money, be in the minds of people, and make the most of one's gifts and talents. "Being on my grind" has become such a staple in pop culture that hip-hop culture pioneer Russell Simmons has developed a Web site called "Global Grind" dedicated to highlighting the lives of the famous, in order to inspire others to live their lives in a way that is meaningful and marked by hard work.

Lil Wayne is one who is respected because of this kind of work ethic. When on tour with a new album, for example, he spends much of his spare time in the studio working on new material. Jay-Z is another grinder, one who has reached one of the highest statuses possible. Jay-Z is a *mogul*: a person of high influence who has built wealth and influence in multiple spheres of life. Jay not only has a lucrative rap career, but he owns a label, has owned a clothing line, is part owner of a professional basketball team, owns night clubs, and has discovered and shaped the careers of some of the most influential artists in the industry. His drive and business savvy have been the blueprint for those inside as well as outside hip-hop culture.

This kind of drive is held in high esteem by men, and yet it is often misdirected and focused. Jesus gives us the example of what might be accomplished with a God-focused and rightly centered drive. Jesus Christ was driven by one purpose and one purpose only—that of His Father. Throughout the Gospels, Jesus speaks of His authority, vision, and mission being motivated by His desire to please His heavenly Father.

John 5:19–20 records this driving passion: "Truly, truly, I say to you, the Son can do nothing of his own accord, but only what he sees the Father doing. For whatever the Father does, that the Son does likewise. For the Father loves the Son and shows him all that he himself is doing. And greater works than these will he show him, so that you may marvel" (ESV).

Verses 30–32 of the same chapter continue: "I can do nothing on my own. As I hear, I judge, and my judgment is just, because I seek not my own will but the will of him who sent me. If I alone bear witness about myself, my testimony is not true. There is another who bears witness about me, and I know that the testimony that he bears about me is true" (ESV).

Running through this chapter (and this is one among many through the Gospels) is Jesus' acknowledgment of His dependence as God the Son on clarity, strength, and purpose from God the Father. God the Father defined and distributed Jesus' purpose. He set the grind for Jesus. Jesus felt so passionately called and committed to the will of the Father that He described what He was doing as imperative rather than optional, as commanded rather than requested:

- "I must preach" (Luke 4:43 ESV). Jesus spoke of His ministry of proclamation not as optional but with the sense of highest urgency and obligation in addition to passion.
- "I must stay" (Luke 19:5). Jesus spoke of His need—not desire—to stay at the house of Zacchaeus. Jesus chose to state His intent in an imperative way in order to display His purpose of sacrificially spend time with the lost.
- "I must bring them" (John 10:16). Jesus felt the divine obligation to gather those not ethnically Jewish to Himself.
- "I must suffer" (Mark 8:31). To Jesus, death on the cross was not optional.

Jesus was not short of drive and purpose. Men, who REALLY follow Jesus, might not have all the details of life, but they will possess in increasing measure this kind of redemptive drive that gives life a dramatic sense of purpose.

Jesus the Overcomer

Temptation is the pressure to yield to influences that can lead people away from God and into sin, an inevitable reality in the life of every man (1 Cor. 10:13; James 1:13–17).[6] Jesus Christ, like every other human being, knew temptation. But unlike every other human being, He never yielded to it. Even when Jesus was led by the Holy Spirit into the wilderness to display the fact that He wasn't sinful like the rest of humanity (Matt. 4:1–11), He showed great faith in God, His Word, and the power of the Holy Spirit to be His strength through such tumultuous circumstances.

Jesus was also tempted to please man. In Luke 11:16, the people in the crowd sought for Jesus to "perform" another sign to prove who He was. Seeing through the nifty cunning of man, Jesus didn't defend His identity, but revealed the lack of faith and perverse desire behind their request. Rather than yielding to temptation to please man, Jesus turned the pressure they were placing on Him back on them.

Don't get me wrong—I like to be right just as much as the next guy. This is at least part of what drives the competitive force in most men. But what we see from Jesus isn't a desire to be right; it is instead a commitment to God and the truth. And it is enough security in Himself and His mission that He didn't have to justify or defend His purpose or importance to any and all comers. How many times each day as men are we faced with the pressure to perform? To justify our identity? To prove ourselves? Jesus didn't give into that kind of pressure.

But the greatest temptation that Jesus overcame was the temptation to avoid the cross (Luke 22:40–46). He knew the strength of this temptation; that's why He asked His disciples to pray for Him. That's also why He went to spend time alone with His heavenly Father. And in this instance, we get a glimpse into the intensity of Jesus' prayer life. Hebrews 5:7–10 gives commentary on this scene:

> In the days of his flesh, Jesus offered up prayers and supplications, with loud cries and tears, to him who was able to save him from death, and he was heard

because of his reverence. Although he was a son, he learned obedience through what he suffered. And being made perfect, he became the source of eternal salvation to all who obey him, being designated by God a high priest after the order of Melchizedek. (ESV)

This certainly wasn't an isolated incident, but it is indicative of Jesus' ferocious ambition to walk with His Father by trusting in Him to overcome temptation. For Jesus, just as it is for us, prayer and vigorous fighting are the means to overcome temptation. Jesus' manhood in this particular instance is awe inspiring; He fought against the greatest temptation imaginable, in regard to His most challenging responsibility, and yet didn't drop the ball:

> He stood only by the power of the Holy Spirit: not by some effortless, Samson-like omnipotence, but by the power of a relationship with God which was moral and personal and which meant that He was invincible in faith, hope, and love.
>
> But in one crucial respect Christ was not like us. He was not tempted by anything within Himself. He was not dragged away by His own evil desire and enticed (James 1:14). There was no law of sin in His members (Rom. 7:23). There was no predisposition to sin, no love of sin and no affinity with sin. The "prince of this world" had no foot-hold on Him (John 14:30).
>
> What then did the devil work on? Part of the answer is that although Jesus had no vices He did have sinless human weaknesses. He could be tempted (and

clearly was) through hunger, though fear of pain and through love for a friend. It is not a mark of fallenness to feel any of these, and yet each of them could generate strong pressure to deviate from the path prescribed for Him.

Foremost among these was the longing for communion with God. Is it any wonder that in the garden of Gethsemene the prospect of losing this communion almost overwhelmed Him. He was not being called upon to mortify a lust. He was being called upon to frustrate the holiest aspiration of which man is capable.[7]

It's profound to consider that Jesus' greatest temptation was not sex, power, or ambition. It was centered on the cross; more specifically, it centered on how, at the cross, there would be a temporary change in the communion and fellowship the Son had enjoyed with the Father for all eternity. Would our temptations lose their attraction in light of the strain of fellowship with the Father that they would bring to us? Would that be true of us as men? I pray it would be. I pray that we would commune with God to the point that the thought of diminishing that communion would cause us the kind of grief Jesus felt in the garden that night and on the cross the next day.

The Sensitive Jesus

One of the greatest taboos in my high school was telling a girl you loved her. Doing so was seen as a sign of weakness, and once that door was opened, you would be at the mercy of the whims of that young woman. In those days, I remember mocking a song by Ralph Tresvant called, "Man with Sensitivity." It went like this:

Listen, baby, don't even waste your tears on an insensitive man.
There's better things for you.
I mean, what you really need is someone who cares,
Someone who's gonna be there for you, someone like me, baby.
Someone with sensitivity.

Ooh, do you understand? can you feel it?
Hey, ooh, naw . . .
Girl, I know it's been hard since he went away
And left you so sad. You cry every day.
Let me kiss your tears, erase all your doubt.
'Cause for you I'm here, you won't be without love.

Don't need a man that'll give you money.
Come on let me show you just what you need, honey.
I got what you need.
Don't need a man that'll treat you funny

You need a man with sensitivity; a man like me.
Someone who can love you, someone who will need you,
Someone who will treat you right, like me, girl.
Someone you can hold at night, someone stable in your life.
Aw, baby, you need a man with sensitivity, a man like me.

Who wants that dude? That's what all of us thought. At least until we realized that every woman wanted that dude. Suddenly, the way we dressed, talked, and walked changed because we knew that the sensitive man could get the ladies. Here's the thing, though—our brand of sensitivity wasn't sensitive at all. It was a mask for selfish desire and a means to manipulate rather than truly empathize.

Jesus, on the other hand, embodies sensitivity rightly— not as a manipulative quality, nor as something emasculated. Rather, in Jesus we see sensitivity as it was intended to be. Matthew 11:25–30 (ESV) reveals Jesus using strong yet laborious terminology to describe His sensitivity to woo the broken into a relationship with Him:

> "I thank you, Father, Lord of heaven and earth, that you have hidden these things from the wise and understanding and revealed them to little children; yes, Father, for such was your gracious will. All things have been handed over to me by my Father, and no one knows the Son except the Father, and no one knows the Father except the Son and anyone to whom the Son chooses to reveal him. Come to me, all who labor and are heavy laden, and I will give you rest. Take my yoke upon you, and learn from me, for I am gentle and lowly in heart, and you will find rest for your souls. For my yoke is easy, and my burden is light."

First of all, Jesus characterized Himself as gentle. In other words Jesus is considerate. Again, this isn't gentleness for the sake of self-interest, but rather a consideration of others due to a deep sense of empathy before them. Jesus considers what people need from the divine in order to relieve them of what is damaging to them. This gentleness and consideration will eventually culminate in His sacrificial death, but remained a mark and characteristic of His life as well as His death.

Second, He called Himself humble or lowly. This characteristic is similar to His gentleness, but it speaks more to the servant nature of Jesus. This characteristic runs counter to what many men view as their role and right. In our fallen state, men tend to view our role as the recipient of service rather than the giver of it. Jesus stands directly contrary to this notion in His sensitivity.

Jesus' sensitivity is particularly displayed in the account of the death of Lazarus. Jesus is described as publicly grieving the death of a friend (John 11:35). Those who were there took notice of how deeply Jesus was moved and responded: "See how He loved him." It would seem that His grief was even good for those around Him, deeply affecting them. Much in the same way, a male who is appropriately and manly sensitive can be profoundly influential on those around him still today.

I remember once in particular while preaching at Epiphany Fellowship, I began to give testimony of how the Lord brought my wife and I through so many trials in planting the church. I recounted how she was sick with cancer as we started the church. The memory was so vivid and the goodness of the Lord was so overwhelming that I couldn't help myself. I began to sob.

As the service ended, I was frustrated with myself— embarrassed at my show of emotion in front of the church.

And then the Lord reminded me of His own sensitivity as a man approached me and said, "Pastor, I was going to divorce my wife, but as I saw your love for your wife in your tears, it reminded me of my love for my wife. Now I am motivated to work on my marriage." I was in shock, but realized that the Lord used those emotions in a way that far exceeded my embarrassment.

Jesus the Jealous Man

Jealousy is one of those human attributes that is usually seen in a negative light. It implies an over-possessiveness concerning someone, something, or someplace. That possessiveness is usually due to fear or insecurity over an anticipated loss. It's particularly heinous, from a human perspective, when it's in reference to a human connection. This internal condition presents itself in a myriad of external emotions and corresponding actions: anger, resentment, inadequacy, helplessness, and disgust all stem from jealousy.[8]

Further, jealousy always involves three persons: self, a loved one, and a rival. Feelings of fear arise in the self when there is a threatened (real or imagined) loss of the affection of the loved one. It is, in fact, often imagined rather than real; and even when it is real, jealousy is never wholly rational.[9] Fear can be accompanied by hostility toward the rival, and both are often intense emotions because the threatened loss strikes at one's self-esteem and narcissism.[10]

Jealousy heightens the human sense of powerlessness, since the jealous person feels incapable of stopping the loss that is about to occur. The Bible talks about jealousy as a "deed of the flesh" (Gal. 5:19–20 NASB). In essence, jealousy then is a passion for one's own pleasure to have nothing in life compete with one's ego. For men, jealousy is almost second nature. It's the reason why we make fun of the guys in high school more popular than we are. It's the reason we hate those who are better athletically, and the reason why we malign those smarter than us. We create chinks in their armor to ease our own insecurities.

But this is jealousy in its corrupted form, marred by the effects of sin. The Bible knows about another kind of jealousy—one that is holy, righteous, and acceptable. It is called a godly jealousy (2 Cor. 11:1–3). God describes Himself indiscriminately as "jealous." This jealousy is a zeal or passion for what is rightfully due Him (Nah. 1:2). This is one of the main differences between godly jealousy and our own.

Our jealousy is almost always connected with something that isn't rightfully ours, but something we feel entitled to nonetheless. On the other hand, all things belong to the Lord. His jealousy, then, is not only acceptable but actually righteous. And when it comes to the glory of God, this is what He is most passionate about—His reputation.

Jesus is passionate about His Father's glory. When the Father doesn't get the glory He is due, Jesus becomes rightfully jealous on His Father's behalf (John 2:17). Jesus wants to see His Father properly represented. When the temple was improperly being used, Jesus showed His righteous jealousy. Not out of insecurity or blind rage but motivated by righteousness, truth, and holiness, Jesus turned over the tables for the glory of God. What an example of manhood! Jesus displayed no fear when it came to making sure that when the glory of the Lord was being misrepresented, He stepped in to bring clarity.

As men we must lead the charge of godly jealousy, but to do so, we must once again understand how Jesus has and continues to redeem our picture of manhood. Jesus could rightly exercise godly jealousy because He had a firm understanding of what had been entrusted to Him. He, as a man, was to project the glory of God into the world. To a lesser extent, so are we. Because we are, we can take the initiative of pushing God's glory in every situation we encounter. And when we see the glory of God being compromised in those situations, we have the right to be in a state of holy rage.

Like David facing down the giant mocking the people of God, we, too, can come onto the battlefield secure in the backing of the Holy One of Israel. And like Jesus in the temple that day, we can turn over tables for the sake of a greater cause and a greater glory. Armed with an overall vision of what it means for us, as redeemed men, to follow in the example of Jesus, we can begin to turn to those specific situations that we need to start upsetting.

CHAPTER 4

Restored Worldview

Michael Vick was a man who knew, from a worldly sense at least, what it meant to have it all. As a top-rated quarterback in the NFL, he had lucrative endorsement deals to go along with an enormous salary. He was feared by opponents, respected by teammates, and loved by fans. But then everything changed.

Due to his involvement in a dog fighting ring, he lost everything—his money, his reputation, and even the game he loved so much. After being released from his jail sentence, he vowed to turn over a new leaf. NFL Commissioner Roger Goodell and other NFL officials persuaded him to pick the Philadelphia Eagles as his team, though it meant joining the team as a third string quarterback. From salary to position on the team, it was by all accounts an incredibly humbling experience. But Vick worked hard and waited for his chance, which wasn't too long in coming after all.

Before the first game, both quarterbacks in front of him had been lost to injury. But when Vick hit the field Eagle fans were not the most excited. Hopes were mediocre at best because no one knew what to expect from someone who had been out of the game for the time Vick had been. But with every dazzlingly accurate pass and every risk defying run, Vick won more and more of the crowd.

In fact, as the game went on, people in Philly began to hope that the other quarterbacks might not actually make it back at all! Over time, Vick's skills on the field earned him the right to be viewed as a compelling leader. As it turned out, that's what the team was really hungry for. It was something more than a great performance; they wanted somebody to follow. And they were not alone.

Our world—our families, organizations, and communities—are crying out for compelling leadership. As we think of compelling leadership—of the genuine desire to follow someone we believe in—we cannot help but think of Jesus Christ. When you look at the passion, life, death, and resurrection of Jesus, it makes you want to follow. It makes you want to crown His greatness. And anyone who still thinks of following this kind of leader leads to a life of boredom simply hasn't taken time to engage in the type of life Jesus has called us to.

The Apprenticeship

In the "reality" television show *The Apprentice*, would-be business moguls fight for the opportunity to be the apprentice of Donald Trump. The prize to the winner of the elimination-style competition is a one-year, $250,000 starting contract of running one of business magnate Trump's companies. At the end of every show, one contestant is unceremoniously dismissed with Trump declaring, "You're fired."

It's a mirror of what happens day in and day out in the world of men as we trip over each other for the chance to be in the same vicinity as power. Surprisingly, though, when offered the opportunity to sit at the feet of the one and only living God as His disciples, we typically don't have the same level of enthusiasm.

Discipleship is like an apprenticeship. The most basic usage of the word in the gospel simply means following. In John 1:37, several disciples of John *follow* Jesus after hearing John the Baptist announce Him as the One he had been pointing to—the One much greater than him. Over and over the phrase points not only to moving forward, but to the abandonment of one's personal pursuits and preferences to follow the compelling leadership of Jesus Christ. This abandonment is illustrated well in Matthew 4:20 as the fishermen "Immediately . . . left their nets and followed him" (ESV). Though these same men might have encountered Jesus in the presence of John the Baptist, this was the moment when they fully took the plunge of discipleship. At that time, they "followed" Jesus; the verb tense indicates a once-for-all action. It's a decision to go all in—to cast their lot fully with Jesus:[1]

> What is more, these early followers of Jesus show paradigmatically that with the appearance of Jesus the Messiah, those identified with old-style Judaism—even if part of a renewal movement such as the Baptist's—

must leave their old religious system and associations behind for the sake of following the Messiah, Jesus. This is as relevant today as it was when the Gospel was first written and read. (Burge 2000:75)

In his classic work, *Long Obedience in the Same Direction,* Eugene Peterson identifies discipleship as a pilgrimage—an ever-growing journey by which the follower is on a voyage with Jesus as they are progressively transformed into His image:

> For recognizing and resisting the stream of the world's ways there are two biblical designations for people of faith that are extremely useful: disciple and pilgrim. Disciple says we are people who spend our lives apprenticed to our master, Jesus Christ. We are in a growing-learning relationship, always. A disciple is a learner, but not in the academic setting of schoolroom, rather the work site of a craftsman.
>
> Pilgrim tells us we are people who spend our lives going someplace, going to God, and whose path for getting there is the way, Jesus Christ.[2]

A disciple of Jesus Christ is one who has renounced himself and pledged his life in a lifetime apprenticeship to the Lord (Matt. 10:39). A disciple is unequivocally committed to Jesus and His goals for his life. Further, this apprenticeship is a transformative one. Those who follow Jesus find themselves being conformed to His image, and it's a transformation they readily and joyfully participate in (Rom. 8:29). This last component of following Jesus is particularly important because, whether we admit it or not, every man is being conformed to something.

Every man has another man they see as an inspiration. We hold these men in high esteem because their image, in our minds and hearts, is exceptionally compelling. It may be a businessman, a professional athlete, a man of power in the community—it could be anyone. But whoever that person is, and whatever gravitas he may possess, he pales in comparison to the true Jesus. The more we recognize the biblical Jesus, His image becomes more compelling and we will want to be like Him. Unfortunately, the more we recognize the biblical Jesus, the more we also see how dramatically short of His example we actually fall. A clear picture of Jesus leaves no room for self-congratulations. But the amazingly good news is that God the Father through Jesus Christ's death on the cross has custom fit our lives to reach the attainable image of Jesus (Phil. 3:12–14).

As active participants in that conformity, we must begin to recognize that as compelling as this journey with the Lord is, there will always be people, places, and things that act as obstructions to this mighty, mighty directive.

Obstacles to Following Jesus

When we walk with Jesus, there will always be things that will get in the way of us being conformed to the image of Jesus. Paul, for example, was thwarted by Satan in returning to the Thessalonians in order to disciple them more extensively (1 Thess. 2:17–18). As I have entered into more and more disciple-making relationships with men, there are two common themes that have emerged as obstacles to following Jesus:

- Unhealthy individuality
- Unhealthy expectations of discipleship

Unhealthy Individualism

All individualism isn't bad. There are things that people can coach us in doing, but even in cooperation with others we will always have to exercise some amount of initiative. But a heightened sense of individuality can be destructive to a man seeking to follow Jesus. Proverbs 18:1 captures our tendency toward unhealthy well: "One who isolates himself pursues selfish desires; he rebels against all sound judgment."

"Isolates himself" is sometimes translated as "one who has separated himself" (cf. KJV, ASV, NASB). A man like this is not merely antisocial; he is a problem for society since he will defy sound judgment. The Mishnah uses this verse to teach the necessity of being part of a community of people who recognize their need of each other and social responsibilities for each other (*m. Avot* 2:4).[3] But this person is ultimately self-reliant and self-focused. They have little or no associations of a friendly kind, primarily due to their egocentrism.[4] They diverge in their own direction, and ultimately find that divergence leading to them not only being emotionally alone, but many times physically alone as well. Carson speaks of this narcissistic individualism in our culture:

In one context, individualism breeds courage, an entrepreneurial spirit, individual heroism, self-denial, differ gratification, and thrift. It may accent values such as honor, and industry. But if for whatever reasons the cultural values change, individualism can easily become a factor that reinforces narcissism, self-indulgence, instant gratification, self-promotion, and greed.[5]

Because such a person is self-focused, the self-denial Jesus calls us to isn't appealing in the slightest. Until we get past this kind of destructive individualism, we won't be able to embrace the kind of interest sacrificing following Jesus calls us to (Phil. 2:1–4).

Unhealthy Expectations of Discipleship

On the other end, we find that there are those who place so much emphasis on human effort that the Christian life rises and falls on the commitment of God's people rather than the finished work of Jesus. The commitment level might be admirable, but it's entirely misguided and can have very destructive results for a disciple. People who struggle with these kinds of unhealthy expectations usually wind up, at some point in their lives, tired and weary of following Jesus. They live in a state of guilt based on their inability to live up to their own expectations. Further, they tend to judge the commitment of those around them, trying to find, in their failures, solace through comparison to others.

Worst of all, the intimacy Jesus died to bring to His people is absent from their lives. They see God not as a loving Father, but as a tyrant constantly telling them they haven't done enough for Him.

A Better Way to Follow Jesus

Life from the Inside Out

Most men, if they're honest, have something about themselves they want changed. Whether it is a physical feature or simply the kind of clothes they can afford to wear, men typically think that if something on the outside changes something on the inside will naturally follow. If we had the right suit, we would be more confident. If we had the perfect physique, we would feel more complete.

See the problem? We assume that real change comes from outside in; it does not. Transformation goes the other direction, from the inside out. When men can avoid the mistakes of over individualization and unrealistic expectations, they can begin to experience this kind of true transformation. True transformation—real, long lasting, life change—is an overhaul of the soul first and foremost.

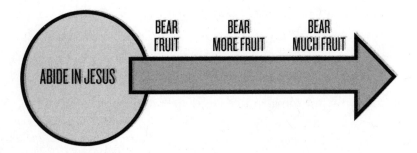

The supreme importance of abiding in Jesus is emphasized in John 15:1–11. When we abide in Christ, He begins to work the change only He can from the inside out. Jesus expects us as His disciples to be on a constant trajectory of growth and change through our connection to Him. When we trust Jesus Christ as our Savior and Lord, that change begins and moves out into all areas of a man's life. This inside-out restoration is the kind of life God has in mind for men.

Sections of a Christian Worldview

Ezekiel 36:25–27 is a good base for understanding all of the Christian life:

> I will also sprinkle clean water on you, and you will be clean. I will cleanse you from all your impurities and all your idols. I will give you a new heart and put a new spirit within you; I will remove your heart of stone and give you a heart of flesh. I will place My Spirit within you and cause you to follow My statutes and carefully observe My ordinances.

In this passage we get a snapshot of the foundational change common to every Christian. God does more, according to Ezekiel, than change us externally; He gives us a new heart. It's a similar description to the way Jesus Himself described life in Him to Nicodemus in John 3, saying that a person must be "born again." Jesus doesn't just change the external and the physical; He goes after the heart.

Through the blood of Jesus our heart is transformed into something new. In other words, all of man's internal components are changed through Jesus—our values, passions, and will are made new. These are the core components necessary for the reorientation of men to God's perspective of life and the world.

Without the gospel no real change will ever happen in a man, for only the gospel can cut and shape so deeply. But through the gospel, we can actually begin to see a man's values begin to change. Values are the driving force behind our emotions. And emotions then motivate our actions. Take any part of the equation out and it doesn't work as it's supposed to.

For example, let's say that a person has much cognitive knowledge, but that knowledge has never fully infiltrated their emotions. They might will themselves to obey, but they won't be happy about it. Remarkably, though, in the gospel, God not only gives us the ability to obey; He also gives us the desire, motivated by values, to do so. Or say a person is reading the Bible and likes, for the most part, what he sees. He considers actually doing what some of the Bible says, but in the end abandons his thought because it doesn't make sense when weighed against what he thinks makes him happy.

All three components are necessary for true change. The Word of God takes root in our minds creating new values, then affections, motivation for the will. This is why when Paul talks about transformation in Romans 12:1 he begins with the renewing of the mind before describing the results of that renewal.

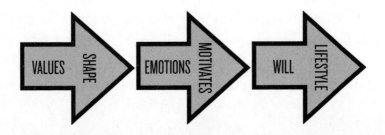

Developing a Biblical Worldview

In our city, orthodox Sunni Salafi Islam is the dominant belief system. In fact, you find many men, now Muslims, who would call themselves "former Christians." Many have left the Christian church because they found the church to be emotionally driven, a place where the use of the mind was discouraged. If this is true, it means that we, as Christians, have done a very poor job of understanding and expressing that the gospel engages a person at every level, including the mind.

In fact, both the Old and New Testaments are filled with truth concerning the nature of the human mind. God cares very much about our mind. As men are restored, they begin to develop a worldview that aligns to biblical values and principles. Their worldview, then, becomes a grid through which these followers of Jesus Christ view, interact with, and understand God, people, and the world (1 Cor. 2:14–16):

> To be a Christian means that God has become our point of reference and framework. "In him we live and move and have our being" (Acts 17:28). As Christians we need to become more and more self-consciously aware of this truth. One way to do this is to follow the apostle Paul's instruction (2 Cor. 10:5) to bring every thought captive to the obedience of Christ or to "think God's thoughts after him." To be a Christian, not in name only, but as one who practices his or her beliefs (which is the essence of a disciple), is to think from a Christian perspective about life and reality. In becoming Christian our life becomes oriented to God

who tells us to "be transformed by the renewal of your mind." (Rom. 12:2)[6]

Looking at the world through this kind of biblical grid is not the natural disposition of humans. Our minds were blinded by the god of this world to seeing the glory of the gospel (2 Cor. 4:3–4). But belief in the gospel of Christ through the power of the Holy Spirit (1 Cor. 12:3) freed our minds from bondage. Now through the resurrected life of Jesus, we are able to see the world based on God's redemptive intentions.

Ephesians 4:23 says that the spirit of our minds is renewed as we take off the old man and put on the new. In other words, the new mind already exists in the life of the believer; we just have to put it on. And this new mind? It's the mind of Jesus (1 Cor. 2:14). With this replacement we are given the capacity to think like our Lord on some level. We are able to comprehend spiritual concepts that aid us as apprentices to Jesus in the skill of living in the world He created to be experienced on His divine terms.

The expansion of the new mind (James 1:21; Rom. 12:1–2). Just because we have the new mind doesn't mean that we have a Christian worldview. Though we have the new mind of Christ when we first believe in Jesus, that new mind needs to be nurtured and applied. The Word of God is the means by which the new mind grows and fights to dominate the thinking and, therefore, day-to-day living of the disciple. We don't just sit around and wait for ourselves to view the world differently. James wrote how the Word needed to be implanted into the soul of the believer (1:21). When the Word is constantly being fed and implanted in our minds, our worldview is functionally changed. *Our engagement of the Word of God includes preaching, teaching, personal reading, and meditation.* Preaching stirs our souls up around the Word of God. A rightly preached sermon, when centered on Jesus and the gospel, nurtures our confidence that we have been empowered to execute what has been communicated to us.

Teaching explains the preaching by further expounding on the principles laid out in that preaching. While preaching stirs the soul, teaching takes us into the depths of what we believe and why. Teaching also provides specific application of the biblical worldview to specific areas of our lives.

Though both preaching and teaching are important, nothing really takes the place of digging into the Word on our own. As we personally and privately study, memorize, and meditate on the Scriptures, intimacy with Jesus is fostered as the Holy Spirit changes our minds and applies the Word to our souls (John 14:26; 1 Cor. 2:9–10).

The execution of the new mind (Heb. 5:14). The end goal, of course, is not just to see the world with a biblical worldview; it's to change the world. It's to live as an influence for Jesus and the kingdom of God within the culture. That's the action, or execution, part of a renewed mind. Peter told us to prepare our minds for action (1 Pet. 1:13) so that we might actually live, rather than just learn.

One of the most prominent areas of our lives to see this relationship between knowledge and action is in our discernment between good and evil. In Romans 12:2, the word for *prove* means "to appraise or to weigh." As we execute the new mind, we weigh our choices, determine which is God's will, and then live it out. As this process is perfected in our lives, it is what distinguishes us as mature or immature in our world-view (Heb. 5:14).

As men, we must grow in this skill. That growth process will come with mistakes and victories, but the important aspect is progression. It is learning. It is growing. Because we have a restored worldview, we can begin to examine more specific areas of life that can now be viewed accurately, and then lived out.

CHAPTER 5

Restored Sexuality

 I remember the alleys well in the complex metropolis where I grew up. Usually these alleys were considered off limits to children because of some of the dark activity that went on there, but that rarely stopped us. One time in particular, I was playing with some friends in the alley and we found some balled-up pieces of paper scattered on the ground. When we opened them up, we discovered pictures of nude women. We giggled at the sight and soon had passed the pictures around to other kids in the neighborhood. Little did we know that that alley, hard as the cement was, acted as fertile ground for seeds planted in us that would take years to surface. This was one of my first encounters with sexuality. And because my first contact was a fallen one, I would need Jesus to reboot me and then teach me God's viewpoint of sexuality.

Most men's first encounter with sex is a perverted one. Whether it was molestation, rape, porn, or playing doctor, many of us have had our "innocence" disturbed. As if being born as a sinner into a sinful world wasn't enough, it is as easy as a couple of clicks on a keyboard for a young boy to move even further down the road of sexual corruption. When we look across the over-sexed landscape of our culture, there is something inside us that cries out, "It's not supposed to be this way!" That's entirely true. It wasn't supposed to be this way.

God's Idea

Let's look back to the very beginning again. If we do, you know what we find? Sex. Not the corrupted version that has infiltrated our society, but sex as God intended it to be. As a matter of fact, sex plays a prominent role in the first chapter of the Bible. From the beginning, God was not bashful or afraid to talk about sex. Instead, He wholeheartedly endorsed it: "God blessed them, and God said to them, 'Be fruitful, multiply, fill the earth, and subdue it'" (Gen. 1:28).

One of the first commands that God gave man and woman was to have sex. A lot of sex. So much sex that the earth would be filled with the product of sex. In the thus far sinless creation, this command is one of great blessing. The Lord "blessed them" before giving the command to fill the earth. "Bless" in this context means "to endow with the capacity to reproduce and be fruitful."[1] Since sex is enjoyable and man and woman would have a natural, God-given attraction for one another, the sex act originally had a dual purpose: reproduction and pleasure. God shows off this innovated brilliance in sex. But then everything changed.

The fall of man in Genesis 3 caused sin and death to permeate all of creation—including sex. The intimately designed relationship between man and woman would forever have a fallen strain on it. Males would try to dominate females as a result of the fall (Gen. 3:16).[2] Women on the other hand would display a disposition of control toward the man. Both of these sinful tendencies are acutely apparent when seen in the sexual terms. In a fallen state, men look at women as potential conquests; women use their sexuality as a form of control and power. What God created for pleasure and reproduction has become a tool in the hands of men and women, a weapon to wield for their own ends.

Boys Will Be Boys

Our society has used a euphemism to describe the expectation of men to have substandard sexual comment to God and family. "Boys will be boys" simply means that we must make space in our expectations for men to be immature; it's just part of who they are. Take it or leave it. So, for example, if a man is cheating on his wife, other women who have experienced the same thing will coach the new victim in functional dysfunction: "Girl, men are just built to have you and others, so get used to it." Even on reality dating shows, women form a kind of relational support group to discuss how they are dealing with it.

Far from a "just let them be" approach, God's Word is very explicit regarding sexual activity:

- Fornication: Sexual immorality with the opposite sex—inside or outside the marriage covenant (1 Cor. 6:18)
- Adultery: Sexual intercourse with the opposite sex—inside the marriage covenant (Prov. 5; 6:24–29)
- Homosexuality: Sexual intercourse with the same sex—rebellion against God's desire for image bearers (Rom. 1:24–27)
- Mental/Visual Lust (Masturbation): Sexual intercourse in the mind (Matt. 5:27–32)
- Bestiality: Sexual intercourse with an animal (Exod. 22:19; Lev. 18:23; 20:16)
- Rape: Sexual intercourse forced on someone (Gen. 34:2; Deut. 22:25–27; Judg. 19:25)
- Incest: Sexual intercourse with certain blood relatives (Lev. 18:6–18; 20:11–12, 17)
- Sensuality: Sexually greedy—debauchery, licentiousness, lewdness, be unrestraint in moral attitudes and behaviors, lacking legal or moral restraints; *especially*: disregarding sexual restraints, marked by disregard for strict rules of correctness, extreme indulgence in sensuality, unbridled lust (Mark 7:22; Rom. 13:13; Eph. 4:19; Gal. 5:19)

The Bible uses the word "fornication" in a general way to describe all of the above. It refers to every kind of illicit sexual behavior—any sexual encounter except that between a husband and wife.[3] "Fornication" is actually where we get the word *pornography*. The term is much broader than mere penetration; it includes looking at, touching, and fantasizing about that which is off-limits.

The Challenge of Porn and Sexual Selfishness

Out of all of the illicit forms of sexuality that plague us, pornography stands above the rest. As a pastor, I do not know any other issue I deal with among men in the church more frequently. The technological socialization is only serving to exasperate the problem. I was brought up in the pre-Internet, smart phone, on-demand digital TV age when pornography was purchased from a bookstore or found crumpled in alleys. Nowadays, sex is readily available at one's fingertips. You don't have to go to an adult shop with a hoodie on; these days, you simply go to the living room. One of the allures of pornography is its accessibility; it promises a purely physical encounter (ironically, though, with an image only). You can be gratified without all the relational hang-ups that come along with it.

But God did not create us to relate to sex in this impersonal way. Although the context of Proverbs 5:1–14 is about unbiblical sex with an actual person, we will see the effects are similar with the use of pornography.

Verses 8–9 state: "Keep your way far from her. Don't go near the door of her house. Otherwise, you will give up your vitality to others and your years to someone cruel." *Vitality* here means strength or manhood. If, says the writer, you choose to go to this woman, you will be giving away years of your greatest sexual prowess and strength. Verse 16 points to the fact that when we seek illicit forms of sexual sin, we give away passions the God calls us to store up for our legal mate. When we unrighteously distribute our God-given passions to illegitimate outlets, we will inevitably be disappointed when we finally come to marriage. Pornography lies to men about the reality of sex and the more we use it, the more we develop a sexual rhythm. When we come into marriage, then, we don't have the slightest idea where to begin in spite of all the sites we've visited and movies we've watched.

Furthermore, we train our passions to be directed toward specific types of women and certain experiences when we use pornography. When we at last get into marriage, we find our expectations shaped by fantasy rather than reality. We selfishly use our wives rather than graciously serve our wives. And inevitably, we become bitter when "she can't do it like the movies."

If our wife, for example, has a different body type than our fantasy women, our oneness has been spoiled before it can even begin. The wife will find herself in an unfair comparison with people neither of you have ever met. The joy the Lord created to be shared between husband and wife find itself in a stalemate.

According to the Family Research Council, married men who are involved in pornography feel less satisfied with their conjugal relations and less emotionally attached to their wives. Wives notice and are upset by the difference. As a result, pornography use is a pathway to infidelity and divorce, and is frequently a major factor in these family disasters. Among couples affected by one spouse's addiction, two-thirds experience a loss of interest in sexual intercourse.

Not only is pornography destructive to marriages; it has a devastating effect in individuals as well. Pornography is addictive, and neuroscientists are beginning to map the biological substrate of this addiction.[4] Users tend to become desensitized to the type of pornography they use, become bored with it, and then seek more perverse forms of pornography. Men who view pornography regularly have a higher tolerance for abnormal sexuality, including rape, sexual aggression, and sexual promiscuity. Pornography engenders greater sexual permissiveness, which in turn leads to a greater risk of out-of-wedlock births and STDs. These, in turn, lead to still more weaknesses and debilities. Child-sex offenders are more likely to view pornography regularly or to be involved in its distribution.[5]

Put simply, it *is* that big of a deal. Pornography is not innocuous; it's a disease, and one that doesn't just go away. What we sow we will reap. Galatians 6:7–8 helps us to understand that there are only two options when it comes to our dark and sinful activities: they will either be exposed, or they will get worse:

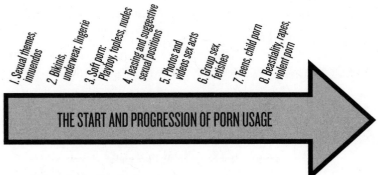

Taken from abattleplan.com.

Rather than turning from this kind of destruction, sexual promiscuity is one of the defining marks of personal identity for most men. Getting as many women as possible (especially if they look good) is a dream for most every man I knew growing up. Even married men applauded those who have the ability to navigate these waters of promiscuity. This is not a new phenomenon. Even in biblical times men were focused on this kind of conquest:

> Prostitutes were often well educated, intellectual, artistic, jovial; they entertained not only with their sexual services, but with stimulating and intellectual discussions, poetry, song, and dance, and witty stories. They combined both fine intellectual sensual pleasures. In Corinth and Megara there were even schools for prostitutes. They were often in service of a deity, called the "foals of Aphrodite."[6]

One first-century man wrote:

> "We have harlots for pleasure, mistresses for concubinage, but wives to produce children legitimately and to have a faithful guardian of daily affairs."[7]

What, then, are we to do? What is powerful enough to even challenge, much less give victory, over such insurmountable temptation? Such societal celebration?

Jesus and Sex (I Cor. 6:18–20)

God created marriage to be the exploration ground for sex. Adam and Eve had the chance to explore what they didn't know. They got to know each others' bodies, senses, and positions. They didn't have the trappings of the preseason game of life that we experience today. At the end of Genesis 2:25, it says the two "were naked," meaning there was no fear of exploitation, no sense of vulnerability.[8] Genesis 2 continues, ". . . but they were not ashamed," which means they lacked the fear of exploitation from their spouse. In other words, they were emotionally free to become one. Jesus Christ came to place all things back in order.

Paul, when challenging the Corinthian church to walk in sexual purity, used the gospel to motivate sexual renewal:

> "Run from sexual immorality! 'Every sin a person can commit is outside the body.' On the contrary, the person who is sexually immoral sins against his own body. Don't you know that your body is a sanctuary of the Holy Spirit who is in you, whom you have from God? You are not your own, for you were bought at a price. Therefore glorify God in your body." (1 Cor. 6:18–20)

First, Paul gave the simplest command: run! "Run" doesn't need exegetical insight; run just means run. Paul commands us to give no occasion for sexual immorality. But this is much easier said than done. All of us have turned off the TV or put down the magazine. We've gotten rid of the Internet, cable, or instituted some type of electronic accountability system. But purely pragmatic strategies don't get the job done for the continued strength. Being commanded to "just stop" would be a frustrating command if left alone. The command alone is not enough.

So Paul adds a consequence of not running. Engaging in fornication will result in an unintended union. Because sex was meant to intimately unite a man and a woman together, whenever this happens between people that are only committed to their lust and not the Lord, they get more than they bargain for in the process.

Genesis 2 tells us that in sex, the two become one. The point Paul may be making here is that sexual immorality causes sexual confusion. Since God created man to be heterosexual, married, monogamous beings, fornication confuses our bodies as well as our souls.

Our bodies, as Paul further points out, are a sanctuary of the Holy Spirit. At this point, he has moved past the command, past the consequences, and is getting into the true motivation for purity. This is a reminder to us that we have truly been made new in Christ.

When you become a Christian, God takes up residence in you through the Holy Spirit. Prior to the days of the New Testament, God showed up at altars, on mountains, in the tabernacle, and Solomon's temple. Ultimately, although David and John the Baptist experienced the presence of the Spirit in their lives in varying levels, Jesus is the first human to be depicted as having been a temple (John 1:14). Jesus promised that those who believed in Him would be endowed with the Spirit's presence as a long-term endowment and blessing. But amazingly, God has chosen to live in us now, not for a brief time, but for the rest of our lives.

As believers, through Christ we have been made worthy to be a place that God is pleased to dwell. In light of this, we must be driven to live a life reflecting who is inside of us. Because of the Spirit's presence, we are members of Christ. Being a member of Christ should make the idea of utilizing for another purpose what Christ has secured for His unique use repulsive. The imagery of the temple helps us to understand this even more deeply, for the Old Testament temple was a special place of holiness and un-defilement. The people of God were to go through extensive ceremonies to honor the temple of the Lord as a unique place because of His presence in it (2 Chron. 5:7). Similarly, when Christ made His home in us, we became that place of holiness and undefilement. And just as an Israelite wouldn't think of barging into the Holy of Holies, so should we have serious second thoughts about our purity.

Furthermore, the presence of the Holy Spirit in us points to the glory of the Lord dwelling in us (2 Cor. 3:18). In 2 Chronicles 7:1, the glory of the Lord filled the temple after the Lord showed His pleasure with the sacrifice. Because of Jesus' death, the glory of the Lord now resides in those who are His. We must not take this lightly.

We must not take this lightly.

When we are in the midst of being tempted to walk in immorality as men, we must consider these truths. We must remember that our bodies have been made members of righteousness not unrighteousness. We should dwell on this and let it motivate us. When we choose sin, we choose to turn a blind eye to what Christ has done in us. But still Paul wasn't done.

Finally, Paul states that "we were bought with a price. Therefore glorify God in your body." This is the trump card

for sexual purity. Remembering His death for us is the ultimate motivation. Christ bought us with the price of His life;
that means our bodies belong to Him and not to us. His death
reorganized how our bodies must be used. If we really name
Jesus as Lord, then we are under divine obligation to walk in
righteousness.

But the million dollar question is how this is accomplished.
Is this just spiritual language or does it work? Motivation without empowerment is empty rhetoric. The great news is that
the death of Jesus is not only motivating; it is also empowering.

Motivation is essentially affection driven by values; values inform affections, and affections drive what we actually
do. Ultimately there won't be any lasting change in our lives
until we accept what Jesus has done on our behalf by faith.
Otherwise, we will write checks with our mouths that our
lives can't cash. Or we will despair in a licentious life without
hope, our consciences remaining riddled with the guilt of our
sin. Jesus' death on the cross can and does remove the guilt of
sin (Isa. 53:4). Because of the death and resurrection of Jesus,
our conviction of sin is not bound up with condemnation.
Instead, we are empowered to repent for real.

Repenting for Real

Out of all the challenges with sexual sin, one of the
greatest ones is repentance. Realistically, most men are going
to have to deal in this area more than any other. We are going
to fall. All of us. And each time we decide to sin (in general) as
well as when it comes to sexual sin, we are tempted to assume
that we have the ability to just snap out of it. To make a better

choice. That our indiscretion was just an isolated incident. But as any addict will testify, the problem runs much deeper. Because it is a deeper issue, we need the power of God to be made new. When we attempt to contrive a solution based strictly on the desire to change, our repentance often times turns out to be counterfeit. When we make promises to God without the power of God, we run the risk of making a rash vow (Eccl. 5):

> A person may purpose and make vows, yet no repentance. We see by experience what protestations a person will make when he is on his sick-bed, if God should recover him again; yet he is as bad as ever. He shows the old heart in new temptation.[9]

Though repentance is at the core of being in Jesus and an essential part of salvation, actually repenting remains for many of us an idea rather than a practice. Though we want to repent—we need to repent—we actually do not repent because we are bound in sin. As time passes and sin persists, we become more and more callous to our action. We need the Lord's power to see our sin from God's perspective.

David found himself at a crucial turning point in life when he was caught in the sins of adultery, deception, misusage of authority, and murder (2 Sam. 11–12). The question for David is the same as it is for us: Will we actually repent? For his part, David owned up to his failure: "I have sinned against the LORD." Note the simple honesty in the statement. There was no blame shifting for David; he did not succumb to the desire to find some sort of justification for his actions:

1. If you would have held me more accountable, I wouldn't have sinned.
2. If my wife was having sex with me, I would be cool.
3. Lord, if You would just take these feelings from me I'd be fine.
4. I was burned-out.
5. I am under a lot of stress and needed an outlet.
6. I had a weak moment.

Rather than making excuses, David wrote Psalm 51, a lasting expression of someone absolutely open, honest, and repentant. The psalm also provides a kind of roadmap to the kind of repentance that lasts.

Acknowledge the character of the Lord. David appeals to an aspect of God's character that he is in need of in his petition—the *hesed* or loyal love of the Lord knowing and appealing to God's character is not a manipulative tactic, but instead an acknowledgment of what God has revealed to be true about Himself. We come to God, then, on His terms as an act of faith that God will actually do and be what He has said He will do and be.

Own our sin. David's prayer is primarily about him and God. There is no blame. No justification. No one else is at fault. Even when David writes of being sinful from birth, he doesn't try to blame his mother or his sin nature, or Adam or Eve for that matter. He never said that Bathsheba shouldn't have dressed (or undressed) the way she did. Instead, there is wholesale ownership of his sin.

Ask for forgiveness and cleansing. He asks the Lord to cleanse him, but to cleanse him in the right places. David knew that his sin was not just a bad choice, but rather a choice that stemmed from some deeper sin of the heart. So in verse 10, he asks for his heart to be cleaned. In essence he is asking for renewed motives and character. Real repentance recognizes the depth of sin and seeks forgiveness and cleansing at that level.

Envision life beyond your bondage. Verse 12 is climactic in the psalm; David asks for renewed satisfaction with the Lord and the desire to be obedient. Read deeper into his request and you find the profound truth that it actually takes God to turn to God. Instead of making empty promises, real repentance recognizes that without God, we won't even want God. We must have this sense of desperation when it comes to being found as bound to sexual sin.

With the power of God, men can truly repent of sexual sin. Once that happens, we can start to return to God's true purposes for sex.

Selfless Sexuality

We are naturally selfish beings. We look out for our best interests and are often willing to step on anyone we need to in order to have our way. This is especially true in something as pleasurable as sex. But in God's design, sex is not just about satisfaction; it's actually about serving. Godly sex is so paradoxical because two seemingly contradictory things are meant to happen at the same time: we enjoy it, but also must be selfless toward our spouse in having it.

Let's be honest—every man wants to have the badge of being good in bed. The funny thing is that this desire often disappears with marriage. But let me say it clearly: God wants men to be good at sex. No doubt.

As those who are called to function specifically sacrificially in the whole of the marital bond, we must even see sex as a part of that (Eph. 5:22–33). Although 1 Corinthians 7 calls both the husband and wife to think selflessly about giving themselves to their spouse, men have the added principle of leading in selflessness in marriage. This principle of selflessness extends to the bedroom as well. Being driven by Jesus' sacrificial death is the principle that men are to live by in a way that marks an exemplary commitment to the wife. Are you getting that? Just as Jesus' death motivates and empowers us as men to live well in other areas of life, it also motivates us in our sexual relationship with our wives. Jesus' death helps you be good in bed!

When we are not preoccupied with our own personal needs, we are suddenly free to see the Lord's picture for our lives. We can look at our bodies as a sacrifice to the Lord first and centrally (Rom. 12:1), and then we can use those bodies in an appropriate manner. There are a couple of ways we need to view sex through this lens of selflessness.

Procreation

Procreation is having good sex specifically to birth and raise godly offspring. The Bible sees procreation as one of the most important reasons for enjoying and having sex. God's first presented purpose for sex is that of procreation and glorification.

When Adam and Eve were commanded to "be fruitful and multiply and fill the earth" (Gen. 1:28 ESV), God intended for man and woman to look forward to having children. It was something to be excited about, not dreaded or feared. Sure, there are all kinds of reasons why this might not be the case for every couple. Perhaps there is an illness involved. Or maybe there are financial concerns. But in our culture, it seems like there are two major extremes in thinking concerning pregnancy: careless pregnancy and over-inhibition of it.

There are those who never consider the practical implications of having children; nor do they consider whether they are emotionally or spiritually ready for that kind of responsibility. Deciding to have children is a life-changing commitment that should not be entered into lightly.

On the other hand, there are those couples who rig their marital life and relations specifically to avoid or chronically postpone having children. Neither philosophy is a good option.

Psalm 127 is a classic passage that provides the right thinking toward procreation: "Sons are indeed a heritage from the LORD, children, a reward. Like arrows in the hand of a warrior are the sons born in one's youth. Happy is the man who has filled his quiver with them" (vv. 3–5).

It's true that times have changed since Psalm 127 was written. And it's true that in those days, children meant greater security for the family. But the principle remains true—children are given from the Lord as a gift to their parents. We should be excited about receiving them as such. As men we must help to recapture a sense of love for the procreation aspect of marriage and sex.

Recreation and Satisfaction

In our culture, this value of sex is exalted to a fault. In the past generations it was ignored to a fault. I used to watch *I Love Lucy*. One of the most awkward things about the show was when it was bedtime they had two separate beds. In that time period, it was taboo for the husband and wife to be seen on network TV in the same bed. Now you can see all kinds of people not husband or wife or someone else's husband and wife sharing a bed with someone. There is a great need to honor the marriage bed (Heb. 13:4) in appropriate ways.

Many Christians tend to shy away from understanding that God created all things to be enjoyed (1 Tim. 4:1–5), including marriage and sex. Understand this clearly: God wants you to enjoy sex. One of the most shocking passages in the Bible on this subject is Proverbs 5:15–19.

Solomon challenges his son to enjoy sex with his wife. Yes, he wanted his son to be committed to one woman. But in the context of the verse, Solomon made several statements that give great insight and freedom to what it looks like to enjoy sex with one's wife. "Drink water from your own cistern," he says. "Let your fountain be blessed," "take pleasure in the wife of your youth," "let her breasts always satisfy you," and "be lost in her love forever." As a married man, this is one of my favorite passages in the Bible.

The man's passion for sex with his wife is described as a fountain of water that has a never-ending resource to pull from.[10] To put it another way, our enjoyment in sex is actually meant to grow over time. God has provided one wife for one man so that our oneness in sex can continue to grow and mature. When married couples find their sex lives to be boring, it's not because they've peaked on the pleasure scale. It's because they have believed the lie from Satan that over time marriage becomes stale. God intends just the opposite—a boundless and regretless freedom in marriage.[11]

Solomon takes it further with sanctified provocative language. He says, "let her breasts always satisfy you" and "be lost in her love forever." WOW! Though Solomon singled out this one part of a woman's body that is meant to satisfy a man, his speech points to the whole of the wife. He desired his son to be lost in her love—to be intoxicated, exhilarated, and captivated by his wife. The term literally means "to swerve; to meander; to reel" as in drunkenness; it signifies a staggering gait expressing the ecstatic joy of a captivated lover.[12] The Bible frees us up to enjoy every aspect of our wife, inside and out.

Single Dudes

"What do I do in the meantime?" If you're single, that's probably the question you're asking right now. To get at the answer, we must first recognize that marriage isn't the cure for lust. In fact, marriage actually opens you up to a whole new slew of issues. But the Lord knew we would have this issue prior to and even into marriage. The principles for dealing with lust are usable for both the single and the married man. I like to call it my three Fs: Flee, Follow, and Fellowship. They're taken from 2 Timothy 2:22, a verse that provides an action plan to fight our sin: "Flee from youthful passions, and pursue righteousness, faith, love, and peace, along with those who call on the Lord from a pure heart."

Flee

As a people called to walk in self-control, the Holy Spirit has provided the ability for us to control our passions. Fleeing is what it says; it's running. And it's through running that we hold onto our legitimate passions. All of us have passions given by the Lord that are good, but how we use them determines the legitimacy of the usage. As one preacher puts it, "There is no easy way to flee; fleeing is ugly." It might not be dignified, but it certainly is effective. Joseph, for instance, when offered the opportunity to sleep with his boss's wife in Genesis, ran in such an ugly way that he left his outer garment behind. But his willingness to be ugly showed his commitment to purity. Sometimes, men, we have to run in an ugly way from opportunities of temptation. When we trust the Lord to strengthen us to flee an opportunity to sin, we experience great joy in denying ourselves illegitimate outlets for our desires. Don't let pride hold you back; run away thanking the Lord that He can lead you through temptation. God never asks us to walk in anything that He hasn't empowered us to do.

Follow

God doesn't just give us prohibitions; He gives us solutions and help. After fleeing, He calls us next to *pursue righteousness, faith, love, and peace.* The more we pursue these attributes the more they will occupy our thinking. And the way we pursue these characteristics is by pursuing the One who gave them to us. Jesus embodies all of these, so following Him is by proxy occupying ourselves with His character. But following Jesus isn't something we can do casually.

The word *pursue* means to move rapidly and decisively toward an objective, *hasten, run, press on*, to follow in haste in order to find something or *run after*.[13] We aren't just running away from temptation; we are running toward the Lord.

Fellowship

As we are running after Jesus, the embodiment of these virtues, we should at some point find others who are doing the same. Together we call upon the Lord out of our authentic need for Him. Although the word for *fellowship* isn't in the text, the principle is certainly present. The New Living Translation expresses the thought well and brings great clarity to the practical nature of the verse. In fellowshipping with other like-minded believers in Jesus, a commonality of struggle and desperation for Jesus causes solidarity and community. We are better together; trust me when I say that you are not alone in your struggle.

Teaching Men about Sex

Another very practical component to restoring men's view of sex involves clear communication. Fathers, pastors, and disciple-makers must make it their business to speak clearly and honestly to men about sex. My good friend Blake Wilson has developed one of the most profound studies I've come across on the matter. In his series called Sex and the Gospel[14] he addresses the fact that for the Gentile church, sex was included as a basic Bible doctrine. In Acts 15:28–29 the early church established that as Gentiles were coming into their faith, they needed a basic understanding of both idolatry and sex. That means the entry-level curriculum for new converts had sex placed alongside the study on Christ, the church, the return of Jesus, sin, and salvation. It was of vital importance that they be schooled in this area because of the challenging worldview that plagued their cities and towns.

Not much has changed. We still need to be teaching men about God's intent for sex. Right now young men learn about sex from the streets, friends, or pop culture; it must instead begin to be the regular practice of the covenant community to make sure the sexual education of the young begins in our homes and churches. It will be a witness to their bodies as well as their souls. Gathering as a group of responsible men and taking the time to be responsible with the hearts and minds of our sons is imperative. If we do, they will forever remember who pointed them to the King of kings as the author of sex and sexuality.

Yes, the temptation toward illicit sexual behavior is all too real. Sexual indiscretion, abuse, and addiction is running rampant. But Jesus has given us the way back.

CHAPTER 6

Restored Vision

 A woman in premarital counseling was asked, "What attracted you to your future husband?" Most men would hope the answer to that question would be that he was sexy and just too fine to overlook. But this particular woman answered with something less exciting. She stated that the main thing that attracted her to him was his walk with God. It may come as a shock, men, but having a passion for the Lord and being willing to walk with Him and your wife through everything that is thrown at you creates credibility. This credibility leads to a sexy kind of trust. Your wife knows and trusts you to lead her, for no matter where you lead her, she knows you'll be seeking the face of the Lord.

Walking with God

Leading a family starts with being in a vital and flourishing relationship with God through Jesus Christ. Jesus' own leadership flowed from His intimacy with the Father. But as men we find intimacy whether with God or others to be a challenge because of our task-oriented natures. Because of our tendencies, we must bring great focus to our relationship with God. This is primarily accomplished through prayer.

I'm not talking about any kind of prayer. I'm not talking about the kind of prayer in public when a man begins to preach to people more than talk to God. Nor am I talking about vain and irrelevant repetition recited around the dinner table just for the sake of saying a blessing. I'm talking about following the example of Jesus in Godward, authentic, focused prayer.

Jesus' Prayer Life

Once Jesus was in a certain place praying. As He finished, one of His disciples came to Him and said, "Lord, teach us to pray, just as John taught his disciples" (Luke 11:1 NLT). It wasn't that they didn't know how to communicate words toward heaven; it was the way in which Jesus did so that was unique. Although Jesus is fully man and fully God, nothing in His life other than His death expressed His humanity more than His prayer life. So what were the specific things that marked Jesus' prayer life? What made it so unique and desirable for His first followers?

- The sense that God is His Father (Luke 11:2)
- A commitment to a particular place (Matt. 14:13; Mark 1:45; Luke 4:42; cf. John 11:54)
- Deep sense of dependence (Luke 22:44)
- Venting outlet (Luke 22:42)
- Talk to God in the most difficult moments (Mark 15:34)

The sense of that God is Father. As we have spoken of previously, the Fatherhood of God is vital in the experience of a man. In almost all of Jesus' prayers, God is mentioned as Father (Matt. 6:9–13; 11:25; 26:42; John 11:41). In essence, Jesus valued the Fatherhood of God so much that it is the primary title He uses when addressing God. Amazingly, He also teaches us to do the same. This is such a great point when it comes to masculine expression in prayer. Therefore, prayer for men should not seem as something that is more natural for women.

A commitment to a particular place. Jesus withdrew to solitary places to pray. We must find places that help our juices to flow when engaging with the living God. A. W. Tozer is said to have had a special spot in his basement where he met with Jesus daily. For me, it's my backyard. Even when it is 20 degrees or less outside, I enjoy engaging with the Lord in that hot spot. It is not as if our signals are weak in other places or that God is more present in one area over another. But there is something significant about setting apart a consistent place for prayer. That is your place. You and your God. Once it's designated, it becomes a place where focus comes more easily.

Deep sense of dependence. To me this is the doozy. As men, we tend to think that it's a mark of weakness to admit our need. We're the men; we should be able to get the job done on our own. But if Jesus Christ was willing to admit His own dependence on God the Father for strength, courage, and direction, who do we think we are to do anything less?

While it's true that on the one hand, God gives us the desire to accomplish things, we must also see from Scripture that what we accomplish is to be done in the strength of the Lord (Col. 1:29). *Fresh Wind, Fresh Fire* by Jim Cymbala has had a significant impact on my understanding of this area of prayer. Cymbala writes:

> Prayer is the source of the Christian life, a Christian's lifeline. Otherwise, it's like having a baby in your arms and dressing her up so cute—but she's not breathing! Never mind the frilly clothes; stabilize the child's vital signs. It does no good to talk to someone in a comatose state. That's why the great emphasis on teaching in today's churches is producing such limited results. Teaching is good only where there's life to be channeled. If the listeners are in a spiritual coma, what we're telling them may be fine and orthodox, but unfortunately, spiritual life cannot be taught. Pastors and churches have to get uncomfortable enough to say, "We are not New Testament Christians if we don't have a prayer life." This conviction makes us squirm a little, but how else will there be a breakthrough with God? If we truly think about what Acts 2:42 says— "They devoted themselves to the apostles' teaching and to the fellowship, to the breaking of bread and to prayer"—we can see that prayer is almost a proof of a church's normalcy. Calling on the name of the Lord is the fourth great hallmark in the list. If my church or your church isn't praying, we shouldn't be boasting in our orthodoxy or our Sunday morning attendance figures.[1]

Venting outlet. As men, we will inevitably experience frustrations and snags in life. Prayer is the appropriate outlet for venting our frustrations to the Lord. The restored man in soul is still in an unrestored world and body, so we must vent to the Restorer of all things. Jesus is described as doing this very thing in Hebrews:

> During His earthly life, He offered prayers and appeals with loud cries and tears to the One who was able to save Him from death, and He was heard because of His reverence. (5:7)

This should be comforting for men—the most perfect and masculine man to ever exist dealt with living in this world and was livid about its state. Jesus went before God with a lot of noise. He was vocal and emotional in His time with His Father. Men need to learn more how to vocalize our "issues" with our heavenly Father.

To that end, David tells us in Psalm 62:8 to pour out our hearts before the Lord. To "pour out one's heart" means to offer up to God intense, emotional lamentation and petitionary prayers (see Lam. 2:19).[2] We must not fear being exposed before the Lord because He is the safest place in the world.

Talk to God in the most difficult moments. Jesus certainly knew about this. When He was in danger of being crushed under the weight and strain of the crucifixion, what did Jesus do? He prayed. He prayed so fervently that His sweat was as drops of blood.

In the book *Men Are from Mars and Women Are from Venus* the author speaks well of the more common tendency of men to go into a "cave" when we are struggling:

> When a Martian (Man) gets upset he never talks about what is bothering him. He would never burden another Martian with his problem unless his friend's assistance was necessary to solve the problem. Instead he becomes very quiet and goes to his private cave to think about his problem, mulling it over to find a solution. When he has found a solution, he feels much better and comes out of his cave.[3]

We must not shut the Lord out. There are times where we can be silent, but we must be willing to cast our cares and burdens on the Lord (1 Pet. 5:7). When we talk to God in these moments, the great news is that He doesn't just sympathize with our weakness as a friend. He also empowers us as the Lord. In fact, relating to God as a friend as well as Lord helps to balance our venting with respect and honor. When we follow the example of Jesus in prayer, we will find ourselves equipped to lead our families and homes in other areas where we are sorely needed.

Decision Making

The type of questions I get the most from men, outside of doctrine, is in the area of decision making. One of the guys I disciple was in a dilemma about whether or not he should take a job that paid twice as much as he was currently making. He enjoyed what he was currently doing, but the extra challenge and pay of the new job was enticing too. In the end, he was completely torn; he wanted to do the right thing, but he didn't know what the right thing was. He's not alone. Men who want to lead their families well will often find themselves in similar situations that demand a life-changing decision be made. And though not every decision is spelled out in black and white in Scripture, there are patterns we can institute into our lives that the Lord will use to help us lead our families through these decisions.

Shaped by being wise. We've already established the need for a biblical worldview; here is where we see that worldview in practical action. The worldview, if you recall, is the grid through which you view everything that happens. If we have that biblical grid in place, decision making becomes the skill to maturely execute what we know and understand to be the will of God. One of the most important characteristics to doing so is what the Bible calls *wisdom.*

Wisdom is rooted in a deep commitment to show God the respect He deserves. That's right—before anything else, wisdom begins with the recognition of the greatness of God. The wise man first and foremost stands in awe of the reality of who God is (Ps. 111:10). The fear or reverential posture of the soul toward the Lord is how one is able to begin to walk in wisdom. In other words, one cannot walk in wisdom or make wise decisions in life without knowing God. Psalms and Proverbs are filled with pictures of this reality. The noun *wisdom (khokhmah)* could be nuanced "moral skill." *Skill* is the ability to produce something of value. The word is used in reference to the skill of sailors (Ps. 107:27), abilities of weavers

(Exod. 35:26), capabilities of administrators (1 Kings 3:28), or skill of craftsmen (Exod. 31:6). Put a moral slant on skill and you get wisdom. Wisdom is skill in living; it is living one's life *so that something of lasting value is produced.*[4]

We tend to think of wisdom in terms of knowledge, but wisdom is far more than the accumulation of biblical information. It's the ability to execute what you know about the information. This execution of biblical information is done with skill, tact, prudence, and God-given and glorifying power. Although the term "wisdom" is used primarily in the Old Testament in reference to human beings, all wisdom is ultimately rooted and grounded in God. Wisdom forms a central part of the nature of God. In wisdom God created the universe (Prov. 3:19) and mankind (Ps. 104:24).[5] True wisdom is described like this in James 3:17: "Pure, then peaceable, gentle, open to reason, full of mercy and good fruits, impartial and sincere" (esv). In other words wisdom isn't just the ability to get tasks, goals, and objectives done, but the character that shapes how and why you do it. It is a biblical philosophy of life put into action.

Direction starts with vision. As a church planter, one of the primary things I was responsible for was the formation and articulation of our vision as a church. The reason why that's so important is that people will not become a part of a new work unless they are confident that the leader(s) have a clear and compelling vision for that work. Maybe even more important, though, is that when we cast vision we follow in the footsteps of our vision-casting God. God has been casting vision from the very beginning. In Genesis 1:26–28, He cast a compelling vision of man and his role in creation. In Genesis 12 He cast vision to Abraham about a preferred future for him even though he and his wife could not have children. He cast vision to Samuel in 1 Samuel 7 about David's eternal house, throne, and kingdom. He cast vision to Daniel about the future of the nation. But His greatest vision casting was that Jesus would die on the cross and restore everything on His behalf (Isa. 53; Ps. 110:1–2). God has endowed us with the ability to cast vision based on what He has already said in His Word.

There should be no visionless men in the church, for vision is the ability and clarity to see God's preferred future through Jesus Christ and the Word of God. Seeing a "preferred future" starts with understanding that since we are in a fallen world, things are not as they are supposed to be. But along with that recognition comes with the resolve and hope that any area of the world can be changed if the Lord Jesus changes it through you.

But rather than having this Jesus-centered resolve, many men today live with little life direction. They live with a kind of "initiative phobia" and "courage paralysis." They are driven almost exclusively by entertainment and only are willing to serve others when they see that service as connected to some personal benefit. When they do find themselves thrust into a role that requires responsibility, they are most of the time unprepared to biblically fulfill that role.

Obstacles to a Healthy Vision

In order to lead their families to make God-centered, healthy decisions, men must have a God-centered, healthy vision. But based on the observations above, I'd say there are three major obstacles standing in the way of this kind of vision in men's lives:

1. Self-motivated dreams (2 Tim. 3)
2. Passion for pleasing others rather than God (Jer. 23:9–40)
3. The unwillingness to unwind current pursuits (Matt. 8:18–22)

Self-motivated dreams. The Bible says in 2 Timothy 3 that men will become lovers of self. To be clear, the Bible doesn't have a problem with us loving ourselves; it even assumes that we do in Ephesians 5:29. The problem is when we love ourselves too much. The biblical kind of self-love is not ethnocentric or narcissistic; it is instead predicated on a fundamental understanding of human dignity. The love of self, then, is motivating to the love of others, not neglect of them. In other words, one of the primary effects of truly loving yourself is the ability to fully give yourself for the betterment of others and the glory of God.

Unfortunately, most men become fixated on self-motivated dreams. Their love of self stops and centers on themselves; they don't see their dreams as mechanisms for the advancement of the glory of God but rather as the avenue for their own power and prestige. To capture true vision, a man must understand the God-centered nature of His dreams and ambitions.

Passion for pleasing others rather than God. This is a challenge for us all. Men are particularly vulnerable to making decisions and forming opinions based on what others will think of them. As men, we love to be acknowledged as "that dude"—being a man's man. We must shift our focus from men to God; we must not be so concerned that our vision has the ears of men but rather is in line with the heart of God. The admiration might indeed come from other men, but it should come not because of our leadership or intelligence or gravitas, but because of our commitment to the Lord.

The unwillingness to unwind current pursuits. For a long time, I didn't want to be the pastor of a church. I avoided the position mainly because I feared that level of responsibility. I knew that to be a pastor, certain other ambitions, hopes, and dreams inside me would have to be put aside. They would have to die. But God is faithful to continue to challenge the direction we're heading (or avoiding) until He gets us where He wants us to be.

Proverbs 29:18 speaks clearly on the issue of clear vision and guidance: "Where there is no prophetic vision the people cast off restraint, but blessed is he who keeps the law" (ESV).

Vision in this context doesn't mean prophecy, but instead refers to the way the people of God were called back to the Word of God when they went astray and acted unwisely.[6] Their unwise actions indicated a lack of resolve or knowledge to walk according to God's vision or guidance for their lives. If, then, this biblical vision is lacking, people tend to run wild. Biblically clear vision sets parameters for our lives.

Without vision, we see a situation like that in Genesis, when man ran wild. We see the same dynamic in Judges 17:6, when man did right in his own eyes because there was no

visionary leadership. Real vision, then, is not some self-imag-
ined dream with a little Bible thrown in, but rather a firm,
biblically centered and motivated purpose that comes straight
from the heart of God articulated in the Word of God.

One of the influential books I have read on the subject of
vision outside the Bible is Andy Stanley's *Visioneering*. He sets
out a practical as well as biblical formula for vision:

Visioneering = Inspiration + Conviction + Action +
Determination + Completion[7]

Stanley expands the formula to point out that vision gives
significance to the otherwise meaningless details of our lives.
As shown in the formula above, vision weaves four things into
the fabrics of our daily experience: passion, motivation, direction, and purpose.[8]

As men we need all of the above in order to not only have a
vision for our preferred future in Jesus Christ, but also to lead
our families and communities to receive and believe in God's
vision for them. This vision provides the *inspiration* we need
in order to lead. *Inspiration* is the drive given by God giving us
the sight of an eternal principle that He has set forth. When
we are inspired, we have strength and passion that transcends
all our circumstances. But inspiration alone cannot stand
alone as we are leading our families to make decisions.

Inspiration must then be coupled with *conviction*.
Conviction is the nagging sense that things are not the way
they ought to be. Paul felt this way in Athens (Acts 17). As
he walked through the city, the Bible says that he became
provoked in his spirit. Paul was upset at the spiritual condition

of the city in light of what he had been inspired to proclaim. Inspiration is the joy and excitement of God's vision, and conviction is the unsettling in soul about the current state of the world in relation to God's vision.

Action must then be added to inspiration and conviction. *Action* is the willingness to actually get involved. It's doing something about your vision. Many of us don't get this far. Most of us have experienced at least moments of inspiration and conviction. While each play a role in the execution of vision, action brings the vision past theory and excitement into reality. Action, for example, is what Jesus took when He cleansed the temple and reinstituted its original divine intent. His zeal for the Lord's glory consumed Him (inspiration and conviction) making a potent mixture that led to action.

Determination is the ability to persevere in the midst of taking action. It is the tenacity and audacity to move forward in the face of seemingly insurmountable obstacles. In Jesus' case, determination kept Him moving toward the cross. Because of His determination, He was able to see the vision of God in His life come to *completion*. Through the power of the gospel we as men have been endowed with the capacity to walk such a path. This cycle is an ongoing process in our lives in every stage. It never ceases but restarts time and time again as we move further and further into fulfilling God's vision for our lives.

Being a Man of Direction

Being a man of vision is also to be a man of direction. Vision gives the picture, but direction is the navigational plan to get to what you see. As we continue to look at the characteristics of wise decision making, we have to recognize direction as one of such characteristics.

Navigating Tough Waters

In my neighborhood growing up, there were men who my mom called, "I could have beens." These were guys who sat on the stoop in raggedy chairs drinking all day and talking about the good old days. They were the star athletes of the past. Many of them showed great academic promise. But without guidance and direction, the past is all they have left. My mother pointed them out to me not to mock them, but to show me what poor planning could do to me. We need a direction. We need a plan.

In the African-American community, a similar dynamic happens in the barbershop. It's full of opinionated black men and is the epicenter for uncut male thought in the black community. The truth is that there are phenomenal ideas shared in that environment—everything from business ideas, neighborhood development ideas, book ideas, to financial opportunities. Unfortunately, not many of these make their way into the planning and directional stage. It's another example of what might have been if only there was a little direction and planning.

Planning is biblical! I would love to say this at least a trillion times. Many well-meaning Christians act as if planning is somehow insulting to the Holy Spirit, as if planning displays a lack of faith in what He can do. But anyone who has actively moved toward a vision knows that apart from the Lord we can do nothing (John 15:3–5). Furthermore, Proverbs assumes that we will plan: "The plans of the heart belong to man, but the answer of the tongue is from the LORD" (Prov. 16:1 ESV). The sense of the word *plans* is considerations. Plans are orderly, purposed, arrangement of ideas with regard to future actions.[9] The term has a military emphasis, as in how a general would get battle plans ready in order to fight well to win a battle. As men we must be willing to set our lives in order. In fact, God holds us responsible for developing an action plan for how to get to where He is sending us.

Did you notice that the text above states that *plans belong to man*? God places on man the responsibility to make plans. He has enabled us with the ability through His wisdom to do so. Redeemed and unredeemed men alike can do this, but redeemed men have an eternal conviction connected to our planning.

With this planning, though, we must recognize the sovereignty of God over all things. Ultimately, what we plan takes God to make happen. Good plans alone don't cause vision to come to fruition. David found that out.

"No"

David wanted to build the temple. It would have made sense for him to do so; the prophet Nathan even told him to go for it. David was a good planner; he thought he had a vision from the Lord, so he put in place a plan to gather the materials and devote resources to the vision (1 Chron. 22). Yet the Lord rejected David as the builder of the temple. Even though David could have done it, even planned to do it, God's answer was no. Instead, God ordained that David's son

Solomon would build the temple. As we see, David aided by doing some of the preliminary planning, yet the Lord saw fit for Solomon to be the ultimate executor of the work. Solomon asked for the wisdom to be able to righteously rule over the people of God. Although this wisdom well exceeded the task of facilitating and administrating the building of the temple, it served him well in that task.

Many times in our lives the Lord will not allow us to execute the plans we would like to implement, even though we have the skill and know-how. We must be willing to accept His decision when the Lord makes it clear that what we are planning is not bad, but not in His will for us.

A Look Deeper

I joined a certain fraternity as an undergrad student. When the potential new members came through the process, we would interview each one about why they wanted to be a member. They responded with things like community service, brotherhood, networking, and many other lame answers. We found that all those benefits could be achieved outside the fraternity; they weren't the real reasons they were there. As we dug deeper, we always found that the true desire for membership was about the popularity that would come with wearing the frat letters. We could see through their initial responses because others had seen through our answers to the same questions. And once men came into the bond, we would laugh about what they initially claimed was their central point of interest.

Being in a relationship with God places us in an evaluative process. We can fool ourselves many times into thinking we have a certain level of honor and purity in our motives. But God sees all. He knows the true motives behind our vision, direction, and planning. Solomon understood this, and he wrote in Proverbs 16:2: "All the ways of a man are pure in his own eyes, but the LORD weighs the spirit" (ESV).

This is a hefty statement. God recognizes that we have a hard time evaluating our own heart and motives. In light of our ability to deceive ourselves, we can and should ask God to be providentially involved in those plans. Man will always believe he is on the right track when we are passionate about something. The word *pure* is used in the Bible for pure oils or undiluted liquids; here it means unmixed actions. People rather naively conclude that their actions are fine.[10] Because what we work on seems admirable, we develop the sense that our motives are undiluted. But, as one of my seminary professors stated, "All of our attempts at holiness are filled with ill-motive." That's why we need the Lord to step in. The Lord who brings plans to fruition will also challenge the place of our heart in connection with the plans.

Specifically, God weighs our motivations. In weighing our motives, God estimates, evaluates, and makes a just determination of the value or quality of our plans.[11] He "gauges" those plans, making an estimate of them by comparing them with His standard.[12] God has a standard for what He wants in the execution of plans. He desires there to be a sense of His goals and passions that drive our planning. Though Christ even covers ill-motives, God wants our hearts to be driven by His passions. When Peter sought to rebuke Jesus for speaking of dying on the cross (Mark 8:33), Jesus rebuked the motive that drove the plan of Peter to have Jesus avoid the cross. Whenever there is selfishness in our planning, God will expose it. The picture is of God placing our motives on a scale next to His passions and desires. When they are out of balance, He exposes them.

This should not be a point of frustration, but a point of comfort. When we are being driven by God's vision rather than our own, it should be incredibly comforting to know that if we have deceived ourselves about our true motives, God will not allow us to persist. He will step in. He will expose. This should give us confidence in moving forward into the actual decision making necessary to truly lead as men.

Empowerment in Deciding

In their landmark book, *Decision Making and the Will of God*, Garry Friesen and J. Robin Maxon speak of the will of God as a sphere rather than a dot. By seeing the will of God like this, the authors emphasize that the Lord has given us multiple tools and oversight in decision making that aid in life direction and planning. They state that the best way to see the will of God in this sphere is in three continuingly smaller spheres: the sovereign will being the largest, then the moral will, and finally the individual will in the middle. The sovereign will is God's divine rule and control over all creation. We see this will shown forth, for example, when God challenged Nebuchadnezzar's belief that his power was absolute versus a power distributed by a higher Sovereign (Dan. 4:28–37).

Second, Friesen and Maxon mention the moral will of God. The moral will of God is that which is revealed in the Word of God. God has given man the responsibility to understand His will, in this sense, through reading, memorizing, and internalizing His Word. David wrote Psalm 119 as a call of responsibility to us for the moral will of God as revealed in the Word. Our ability to make decisions is most connected to this will. Man must be willing to be exposed to the richness of the Word of God to know the will of God for our lives (Col. 3:16). When this will is deficient in our lives, we will often find ourselves at a loss of basic, intermediate, and advanced direction. Without the moral will as revealed in the Scriptures we cannot plan well at all.

Finally, comes the individual will of God. This aspect of God's will is a real thing, but we often have an inflated view of it. We tend to be driven by individual will because we would like to think of ourselves as special—that God has plans for us that don't apply to anyone else. While that's true in a sense, it's also true that 90 percent of what God wants us to do has already been revealed. Furthermore, the liberating power of the gospel gives us a garden of freedoms that go under the banner of the sovereignty of God. Still, we often find ourselves claiming to be at a loss about what God wants us to do. Perhaps, though, we are too focused on these decisions and should be more concerned with our overall obedience to what we know to be true in our lives:

"The problem is not the lack of God's involvement in our decision making. The problem lies in our failure to properly integrate the Bible's instruction on decision making with the larger framework of its teaching on a personal relationship with God. Making decisions is but a slice of our walk with God. If we are to properly interpret the details of our lives, we need to have a more complete understanding of what it means to "walk by faith, not by sight." (2 Cor. 5:7)[13]

Our understanding of these wills is important so that we will not view any of them exclusive of the others. All are important and connected. In relation to decision making, they all aid in our trust of the Lord in knowing that He involves Himself in our planning and holds us and empowers us with the ability to make decisions. As true as the responsibility for decision making is for all believers, it is even more for men. If men are called to be leaders in the home, we must grow in our skill of it (Eph. 5:26, 29). Because God allows us to have a wife and children (Ps. 127), God will hold us responsible for our households. When Joshua stated that he and his house would serve the Lord, he was giving vision and plans for how his house would run. It is a statement of the sovereignty of God, moral biblical culture of the home, and the individual decision to participate in both. This kind of leadership involves all three aspects of God's will at some level.

The Encouragement

Man is given the responsibility by God to bring our work or planning to the Lord. This is where we come out of the vacuum of personal preferences divorced of God's eternal ends. Proverbs 16:3 calls us to commit our work to the LORD, and promises that if we do, our plans will be established. "Commit" means to roll, as in rolling one's burdens on the LORD. The same idea is found also in Psalms 22:8; 37:5; and 55:22. The idea is one of complete dependence on the LORD. This is accomplished with a spirit of humility and by means of diligent prayer, but the plan must ultimately have God's approval.[14] As we have the approval of the Lord, we must diligently work on the approved plan. The Lord establishes the plan because it is in His will.

When we are seeking to establish the vision and plans of the Lord, the following outline is helpful:

1. Pray
2. Ask God for visionary and directional clarity
3. Write down the vision
4. Plan and strategize what it will take for the plan to come to fruition
5. Continue to seek the Lord's face
6. Seek godly counsel
7. Make the necessary revisions
8. Work the updated plan with much prayer
9. Thank the Lord for bringing different aspects of the vision and planning to fruition.

As I "sensed" a call to ministry, I sought the Bible to find clarity. As I read on the call of many, I compared my experience with theirs. In addition, I began to look at what God wanted from servants and pastors in ministry and began to seek the ways in which this could be fulfilled in my life. I placed myself in the position to live in light of what I saw in the Bible and "felt" the Spirit at work in my heart. I looked at the character in Joshua, Jeremiah 1, 1 Timothy, 2 Timothy, Titus, and 2 Corinthians, and the Lord stirred my heart and opened doors. I received tons of counsel and was encouraged in Christian community about how to proceed. Praying and fasting helped tame my flesh to hear the Lord speak in principle more deeply though the Bible and counsel. Over time, the Lord has been helping me to sharpen this idea of being a directional man. That last part is key—this is a learned skill that must be vigorously sharpened over time.

Practice makes perfect—or at least it makes better. Whether it is thinking through how to provide for our family, what career path to take, where we live, what church to attend, or how to parent our children, it will serve us well to be found actively seeking the face of the Lord so that we might become better decision makers. Specifically in leading our families, they will enjoy our journey with them and the Lord as we follow Him and see His heart and hand all the days of their lives. The soul of our wives will be at great rest knowing that her undershepherd is willing to go to great lengths to align the family with the heart of God. It is an incredible honor to hear your wife say, "My husband follows God."

So how do we stay sharp? By seeking the face of the Lord. By practicing the presence of God, we live the whole of our life in prayerful openness to the Lord (1 Thess. 5:17).

Final Thoughts of Planning and Decision Making

There are some definitive statements Friesen makes as we conclude this subject that deserve our meditation.[15] These can act as basic guiding principles for men to utilize in personal and family direction.

God has provided the resources for making decisions. God has given us everything we need for our spiritual lives in general as well as vision and planning (2 Pet. 1:3). In granting us these resources, He has given us the ability to execute as well.

As we work through the process of arriving at the decision, God is continually present and working within us. Paul reminds us that it is God who works in us, "both to will and to work for his good pleasure" (Phil. 2:13 ESV). This is a comforting statement as we plan and make moves. The gospel makes forgiveness available if we go off track as well (1 John 1:9–2:1). As we grow in the Lord, the focus is more on our personal growth and the growth of those around us than the working of the plan itself.

It is God who sovereignly opens doors of opportunity for us. Paul knew and understood this principle well. In Acts 16:6–10, Paul experienced the Holy Spirit forbidding him from speaking in Asia, but instead directing him toward Macedonia. Just as preaching was the will of God for Paul, so was the "where." God directed his path (Prov. 3:5–6) as he trusted Him as the author of his journey. When we recognize this, we will not become bitter and angry because God closes doors in our lives for a time. Many times He will direct us another way. In leading a wife and a family, this closing of doors doesn't squelch our credibility; it confirms it. The family will hopefully learn and understand that their life isn't about merely following the will of Dad or hubby, but that of an eternal father.

As we planted Epiphany Fellowship, I wanted to live in the neighborhood of the church. The Lord didn't open the door for it to happen. A few years later the Lord began giving us a great missiological burden for moving closer to our target area. We didn't have the resources to close on our current house nor the ability to buy a new one in the recession. But the Lord provided exactly what we needed and He opened the right door even if it wasn't the one we thought. My wife to this day sees the Lord's hand and acknowledges His work in not only getting us into the house, but also giving us some amenities that we would not have had otherwise. It is exciting to watch the work of the Lord in key opportunities to reflect His name.

Along the way God utilizes the circumstances and the very process of decision making to change our character and bring us to maturity. Peter would attest to this one. In Acts 10 he was given the opportunity to take the gospel to the Gentiles. God overwhelmingly worked in the house of Cornelius and saved many. As a result of this experience, the Jerusalem counsel affirmed that God was at work among people who many believed to be outside of the reach of the gospel. But God worked in Peter and the church in Jerusalem to grow their understanding of God's plan for all the nations of the earth. Peter's decision to follow God's direction to Cornelius wasn't just for the sake of Cornelius; it also served to change Peter and the entire church, by bringing them all closer to maturity.

CHAPTER 7

Restored Family

 As the man grows in relation to his commitment to Jesus and develops a trajectory for his life based on the grace of God, he becomes more and more eligible for marriage. Early on in my ministry, I was a pastor at a church in Houston. I enjoyed the vast amount of pastoral experience that I received shepherding the flock at Good Hope Missionary Baptist Church. Dr. Cofield and the congregation were extremely gracious to me as a recent seminary graduate. Ministering there helped me thaw out from my personal immaturities I had acquired through my prideful time as a student. I got to do thirty-two funerals in one year, performed my first wedding, taught senior Bible study, developed ministry calendars, visited the sick and shut-ins, loved and disciplined the wayward, led praise and worship, started sixty small groups, sharpened my preaching and teaching skills, developed premarital classes, and much more.

During that period, it became clear to me how important it is to develop men and prepare them to be husbands. I learned and am learning that if you prepare men to be Jesus-loving men, they will make great marriage material. Unfortunately, many men develop an entitlement mentality toward marriage. We think that since we "put a ring on it," that was sacrifice enough. It's like in the back of our minds we say, "I could have stayed out of that commitment, but I chose you." That disposition creates a cynical relationship with men and their spouses. We must have a gospel-driven heart when it comes to being a leader of the home.

Jesus' sacrifice is the most attractive part of His life. I don't want to be a reductionist, but the fact that He left heaven and took on an additional nature, died on the cross for us, and was raised from the grave makes Him an extremely compelling leader. When you look at a passage regarding marriage like Ephesians 5, it is impossible to ignore the sacrifice-soaked principles in the text. We can go through all of the principles of leadership we want, but what makes Jesus a compelling leader is His willingness to die.

I am a big movie buff. The latest King Kong movie that came out a few years ago was a funny and insightful movie. The main female character was named Ann, the woman that King Kong was obsessed with. As you watch the development of the relationship of Ann and Kong, the director wove the principle of sacrifice in the film. King Kong fought off two dinosaurs who wanted Ann as lunch. With one hand or foot he fought hard against these impending enemies, but at the same time with the other free hand or foot carefully and masterfully held and protected Ann during this crazy battle. He came away from the battle battered, bruised, and fatigued, yet he was relieved that he had protected her. Although they were in the midst of this battle, she felt loved, protected, and handled gracefully.

On the cross Jesus does the same. Being a sacrificial lover and compelling leader is what motivates the church to serve Him. In Ephesians 5, Jesus is called the head of the church. He earned that title by saving the church. In other words Jesus is the Lead Servant in His relationship to the church. Jesus leads through sacrificial initiative. Fellowship Associates and Fellowship Bible Church Little Rock helped me with one of the most powerful definitions of leadership: "Leadership is taking the initiative for the benefit of others." This is a phenomenal summation of the role of Jesus in the life of His bride, the church. Christ earned His place as husband and now motivates the church to voluntarily submit itself to His Lordship.

Loving Our Wives

The husband is exhorted to reflect Jesus' sacrificial leadership in relation to his wife in verse 25. According to Paul, the primary way this leadership is displayed is through love. Then, out of love, the husband lovingly leads the wife through aiding her spiritual growth and through care.

Love

Our culture "loves" everything. We are in love with being in love. But in Paul's day, the word wasn't thrown around so easily. In fact, his command to husbands to "love" their wives was unbelievably radical. In telling husbands to love their wives, Paul went well beyond the familiar Greco-Roman codes. In that society, the command might have been something like "Husbands, rule your wives." Instead, Paul commanded not just an affection for the wife, but the willingness to sacrifice self for her comprehensive spiritual benefit. This doesn't mean that a husband should build life around his wife's preferences, but it does mean that he should consciously live his life considering her spiritual development. Practically, this means the husband should be making decisions and setting priorities through asking and answering questions like the following:

- Is she the main supporter of the family, financially, emotionally, or even physically?
- Is she leading the family while you lay passive on the couch?
- Does she struggle with submitting to you because you die to her but not to yourself?
- Are you further developing yourself spiritually, financially, and emotionally, to cover her comprehensively? Or are you in a place of stagnancy while your wife is dying on the vine struggling to make sense of your passivity and narcissism?

These are real-life questions. Love must have these practical components and considerations. Unfortunately, most of us treat the love of our wives in an extremely abstract manner. "Of course I love my wife" we say, but that love rarely makes it past the point of words and theory.

When Paul, in this passage, says that the relationship between a husband and a wife is a profound mystery, but that he is actually talking about the gospel, pastors find a point of theological excitement, but have trouble translating that theology into real action points in marriage. In 1 Peter 3:7 (ESV), Peter refuses to let the issue remain one of theory. He gives the husband an extremely practical yet theologically weighty principle for loving his wife: "Live with [her] in an understanding way," or in the KJV "according to knowledge." As men we need to become students of our wives. That means understanding what sets her off emotionally, her needs, her passion, and her preferences. Paul develops a similar idea in the remainder of Ephesians 5, as he gives two outworkings of truly loving our wives.

Spiritual Growth

"Washing of water by the word" (Eph. 5:26). That's the phrase Paul used both about what Jesus did for His church and how the husband might follow His example in relation to his wife. This means to bathe her in the Word through communicating it to her. The same idea is expressed in Titus 3:5 of the Holy Spirit's work in washing us with the blood of Christ to take us from spiritual death to spiritual life. Jesus has done this at the point of salvation of the wife.[1] The gospel, then, is the ultimate way in which the Word has made her clean, just as it has made the husband clean. But as husbands and restored men in marriage, we are to continue this work as we work for the continued sanctification of our wives. We are to *administer gospel-centered words from the Bible* to aid in the work of God for her life and growth.

Although we will have to communicate challenging words from God at times as the spiritual leader of the home, the bite of condemnation must be absent from this vulnerable bathing. The point is not some kind of brutal, judgmental, theologizing, but careful and loving instruction that feels like a soothing bath. That's what sanctification ultimately is. It is the setting aside of a unique vessel for the Lord's specific use. It's what Jesus did for the church, and what the husband cooperates in for the sake of his wife:

> Sanctify them in the truth; your word is truth. As you sent me into the world, so I have sent them into the world. And for their sake I consecrate myself, that they also may be sanctified in truth. (John 17:17–19 ESV)

The husband's role is to reflect Jesus' self-denying death as he helps the spiritual growth of his wife. The end goal is for his wife to be set up to win in every area of life to the glory of God. Men, if your wife is lifeless, uncommitted to the Lord, spiritually docile, and ineffective in her role as a wife, you need to consider not what is wrong with her, but rather what *your* role is in her being in that state. It doesn't all fall on you, just as it's not Jesus' fault if you aren't moving forward spiritually. But you must think long and hard about whether you have truly died to yourself enough to empower your wife to the glory of Jesus. How does your life set your wife aside to uniquely love and serve the Lord in her God-ordained role?

The way this is fleshed out is unique in every relationship. In my own marriage, I have had to learn to give my wife biblical nuggets that drive her more deeply into the Word of God for herself. In the past I would develop these elaborate theological plans for her, but she wanted and needed more pointed biblical referencing. In living with her "in an understanding way," I have had to recognize her learning patterns and preferences and take that into account as I actively plan and pursue *how* to most effectively shepherd her as her husband. Because each marriage is as unique as each woman, we can't approach this haphazardly. We need a plan for the spiritual growth of our wives. The following are some suggestions about how to develop that unique plan in your own marriage:

1. Get a visionary picture of what the Lord wants a biblical woman to look like.
2. Pray for her growth.
3. Expect that the Lord is going to grow her.
4. Pray for the strength to lead her in a loving and caring way.
5. Develop goals and objectives for her development based on Scripture.
6. Read solid books on biblical femininity.
7. Do not be overbearing toward her pace of growth.
8. Load your soul with truth so that the Spirit has something to pull out of you.
9. Learn to minister her through listening. Sometimes women talk through their issues knowing already what they need. They just need our understanding to listen. Telling her what she already knows can lead to exacerbating her frustration and create a wall in communication.

10. Repent of your sin without bringing up her sin.

11. Set her up to win. Make sure she recognizes that you are for her. As you develop plans, facilitate her ability to walk in her role as a wife. That could mean money, resources, and time to develop great community, just to name a few.

Care

This is the second outflow of love for our wives that Paul mentions. Caring for our wives means nourishing and cherishing them. *To nourish* literally means "to provide food or to feed." *Cherish*, on the other hand, literally means to impart warmth; hence cherish, comfort, tenderly care for.[2] Caring, then, means comprehensively providing for the needs of your wife. This encompasses finances, emotions, security, and all things otherwise. It means making sure that you have a budget in place, are saving for the future, and know what she might be concerned about on a day-to-day basis. Men, nourishing your wife means setting an environment where she feels safe, secure, and at ease so that she can flourish. The manner in which you set this is where cherishing comes in. It's the spirit of the nourishing. You don't do these things bitterly or begrudgingly; you take on that responsibility with great joy and care, and you find fulfillment in making sure your house is in order. Both words help explain the character that the sacrificial leader has in mind when leading.

Pastors Set the Tone for Restored Manhood

Growing up in what was at the time a predominately African-American city, I was surrounded by Black Nationalism. The images of hip-hop, the Nation of Islam, Al-Islam, Black Hebrews, sports players, and black intellectuals defined what it means to be a man. I saw the men at church, conversely, as soft, too emotive, anti-intellectual, and unskilled. The men's groups were filled with clichés and "Christianese" that I viewed as formality that lacked spirituality. I found myself looking to those cultural images of manhood instead, for they offered a much greater appeal. It's not that I doubted the church men's love for Jesus; I just struggled with the lack of husky masculinity that I saw in the leadership of the competing spiritual entities.

In the Bible though, I have found the opposite. I saw that Jesus appointed manly men to lead the church and set the tone for manhood in the body. The earliest church leaders were dudes. When Jesus prayed all night to the Father, asking for whom He would include in His first group, the Father delivered religious skeptics, businessmen, Hebrew fundamentalists, thieves, thugs, a shady government worker, radical Jew, mama's boys, and spoiled rich kids into one crew to represent Him. Once redeemed, their cultural manhood was brought under the cross and raised with Jesus. They retained their quality of manliness; they just had it in a redeemed state. This isn't to say that manhood is to be reduced to cultural stereotypes, but the truth is that people know a man's man when they see one. Tamed by redemption, it will serve the gospel

well to have these men present in the church. Paul knew this
to be true.

Paul implemented manly men as the earliest church leaders. He left Timothy in Ephesus to challenge men who were
destroying the work of the gospel in church. In 1 Timothy 1:3
Paul tells Timothy to charge or order the men who are domi-
nating the teaching with false teaching. This kind of confrontation would require a manly man, one unafraid to confront
issues head-on and face-to-face. Not only that, he instructed
Timothy to set the pattern for manhood and church govern-
mental direction by appointing qualified male shepherds to
lead the church. Inferentially, these men would give young
men a vision of manhood to look forward to and the young
ladies a marital image of a husband to choose. Today, in our
fatherless culture, shepherds in the church function as spiritual fathers to those who lack a godly image of a man in the
home and world. How can they do that if they don't set the
pattern of what it means to be a man themselves?

Dr. Tony Evans was the first black man that I saw in the
church with strong degrees in theology, that led his family
well, preached the Bible expositionally, and placed Jesus above
himself in the church. I can remember many of us being mes-
merized by the grace of God on the way that he ministered the
Word of God and answered questions apologetically. When I
saw his theological library, I was blown away by the breadth
of material that he had on his shelf. Dr. Evans showed me, and
many others, what a real man looks like in church leadership.

In 1 Timothy 3:1–7, Paul lays out three areas that act
as character gauges for those wanting eldership: personal

character, family character, and community character. These areas not only mark church leaders, but also give us a picture of manhood that all men should find helpful in their walk with Jesus. This is not intended to be an elder qualification manual, but it is clear that men need to *get* how to be like Jesus from their pastors. It is imperative, then, that pastors and church leaders fully understand what the Bible says are the essential qualities of manhood if they are to lead young men to become mature men in the faith.

Personal Character

The area of personal character is central to what it means to be a man. Specifically, Paul says that these men must be above reproach. Being above reproach means to have moral conduct "blameless, above criticism, without fault, unimpeachable."[3] That means no one can bring a charge against you personally as well as professionally; you have integrity in all that you do. Just as God's glory permeates His attributes, so does being above reproach have a similar feel to the elder's characteristics. If church leaders exemplify this character, their congregation will follow. When there are biblical standards that drive the force of the church in character, men respond by seeking to align themselves with such character.

Family Character

One's reputation inside the home is a good barometer for one's ability to be in leadership. Paul specifically mentions two elements of family character in this text: household management and marital faithfulness. A "one-woman man" points to marital faithfulness, specifically in the area of sexuality. I say this as humbly as I know how: marital unfaithfulness has become one of the worst marks of the pastoral ministry. Rarely a week goes by when an issue of sexual unfaithfulness isn't uncovered in the leadership of the Christian church. And that unfaithfulness has a trickle-down effect.

Men in the church have used the immorality in the pastorate as a means to justify their unfaithfulness. It's not that every man doesn't make his own choices; he certainly does. But unfaithfulness in the pulpit clearly has an impact on unfaithfulness in the pew.

When a church leader loves his wife and has eyes only for her, men are inspired to love their own wives. Unfortunately, many times men in church leadership are allowed to be passive in their love for their wives. But over and over again, the Bible exhorts men to be unashamed in our love for our wives (Prov. 5:18; Mal. 2:14–15). Men, with pastors in the lead, should fight to pursue their wife. We should be so filled with stored up passions for our wife that she gets to be the focus of the love that God created her to receive from us.

On a larger scale, pastors are to manage their homes. That means to lead their homes. Though I mentioned this earlier, there are several aspects to this kind of leadership in the home that need to be broken out further. Leadership in the home includes the following:

- Ministry of presence (be home, engaged and interested)
- Ministry of spiritual formation
- Ministry of gospel promotion in the home

- Ministry of family vision (setting a trajectory for family that is centered on Jesus): Where are you as a leader taking your family? Does the family identify that direction as the goal?

Ministry of presence. It is almost embarrassing that such a practical point must be mentioned, but men must be at home. Men must be present. When children grow up, they remember certain details about their upbringing. Many times those things are major details, like vacations and big-time punishments. But one thing children never forget is if their father was present in their lives and what that presence was like. When men speak of their father being absent or not around, it is an embedded memory. Presence in the home is the bedrock of being in a family. This isn't just about something like "family worship"; it is instead a comprehensive passion to be present in the lives of our wives and kids. Jay-Z spoke to GQ magazine about this very topic.

With the arrival of his daughter (or son) just around the corner, *Jay-Z* is likely thinking a lot about being a first-time father. But the self-made mogul is clear about one thing: he'll do things differently than his own dad.

In the December issue of GQ, Jay admits that being abandoned by his own father at age 11 has left him "a little paranoid" about being a dad himself. "I don't think any person . . . goes into a relationship thinking they aren't going to be there," he says. "You just never know."

"If your dad died before you were born, yeah, it hurts, but it's not like you had a connection with something that was real," he explains. "Not to say it's any better, but to have that connection and then have it ripped away was, like, the worst. My dad was such a good dad that when he left, he left a huge scar. He was my superhero."

It wasn't until more than 20 years later that Jay-Z, then 33, reunited with his father. "[I talked about] what it did to me, what it meant, asked him why. There was no real answer. There was nothing he could say, because there's no excuse for that. There really isn't," he said. "So there was nothing he could say to satisfy me, except to hear me out. And it was up to me to forgive and let it go."

As for what type of father Jay will be to his little Hov? "Hopefully one that can have conversations," Jay-Z tells E! Online. "Your child could come to you and have any type of conversation. I always hope for that kind of open relationship."[4]

The ministry of presence must be an absolutely primary part of a restored man's agenda. As Psalm 127 articulates, a man is to labor in his home. Applicationally, this laboring includes providing, visioning, praying, instructing, and much more. None of that happens without presence—the active involvement in the life and development of the family.

A man must, then, actually enjoy being with his family. They must not be a necessary evil or a source of major frustration, but the people with whom we have deep and rich relational commonality. Be home, men! Our presence sets the culture of the house. Jesus has restored the ability for the man not to be a passive and/or aggressive presence in the home, but one that impacts the life of one's wife and children. What should the memory of a father and husband be like for his family? This is the sort of burning question men should think through each day in the home.

Ministry of spiritual formation. Planning for the spiritual growth of one's wife and children cannot be overstated. We must be able to biblically work through God's vision for them. As it pertains to the children, we must seek to root them in the gospel as much as it depends on us by saturating them with a biblical grid.

Ministry of gospel promotion in the home. Whether we are discipling, challenging our wife, having fun, or instructing, the principles of the gospel must permeate all. This isn't an easy priority to have before us. Many times when I am discipling my sons, I become so agitated by their actions that I forget the gospel. I forget mercy, love, grace, and, most of all, I forget I am supposed to be helping them to understand forgiveness. Without the gospel, I am only projecting behavioral modification. Change of heart must trump mere change of behavior. Therefore, the goodness of God through the gospel must trump all other philosophies in the home.

Ministry of family vision. The family must know where the family is going. We are not on some aimless journey of spirituality, but on our way to God. Because we are on our way to Him through Him and with Him (Titus 2:11–15;

Matt. 28:20), there is divine reasoning and meaning in every day of our lives. As we have discussed, having biblical vision gives the house biblical grounding and purpose. Vision keeps us from running aimlessly. The culture of biblical vision running the household will give the family a great sense of gospel hope. Remember, Jesus has vision for His family. Jesus has prepared a place based on His vision for us to spend eternity with Him (John 14), has an image that we are conformed to (Rom. 8:29), and will bring it to fruition (Rev. 19–21). To follow His example means we project a similar vision for our own families.

Community Character

In addition to personal character and family character, Paul advocates for character displayed in the community. The reputation and influence of a man in the broader community is important. In the context of eldership, pastors are to be men of great respect. That doesn't mean everyone has to like you; far from it, in fact. It's okay to be disliked, but it's not okay to be disliked for the wrong reasons.

This reputation and respect should extend from Christians into non-Christians as well. In fact, Christian men will do well to be respected even among those who reject the gospel. It's this respect that can ultimately lead to opportunities for the extension of the gospel. In the Sermon on the Mount, Jesus stated that the people of God must have an exalted witness among the heathen (Matt. 5:13–16). The result of men being the men they are called to be is God getting the glory from Christians and non-Christians alike (1 Pet. 2:12).

In my city, the character of the men make or break the missionary viability of any religion among the lower class ethnic people groups. One of the reasons my own city respects Islam so much is because of the character of the men. They are the ones seeking economic development in poor communities. They are the ones seen with their children and women in public, and they are therefore the ones with the greatest religious presence in the community. We must have an exuberant passion to see this change. Men in Jesus should be the best of men in our cities and towns. If Jesus has restored manhood, then we must be the best fathers, husbands, businessmen, leaders, servants, lovers, intellects, artists, and visionaries.

All these characteristics should abound in the leaders of our churches. If they do, they will soon abound in the male members of our churches. If we turn to another of Paul's letters, this one to Titus, we see more practical instruction for both younger and older men as Paul attempted to institute leadership in the churches he started.

Instruction for Younger Men (Titus 2)

Interestingly enough, the Bible makes a distinction between the age groups of the genders in the church. In Titus 2, Paul gives some helpful premonitions of what younger and older men should exemplify. Of all things Paul might have said are important characteristics for a young man, the one he zeroed in on was self-control. The force of the term means to be prudent, "reasonable, sensible, serious, and keep one's head."[5] The same term is used in verse 12 as a general quality of all believers. But for the young man, not much could be harder, and therefore not much would distinguish a young man in Christ more than a self-controlled life. The principle is so powerful that Titus is called to be an example to these young men.

> The scope of its application, "in everything," suggests that this is to be the fundamental characteristic of their outward conduct. Moreover, the self-control called for is equally measured to pull these young men out of the sexually and otherwise indulgent lifestyle that was the norm in Cretan culture. As throughout the passage, Paul regards this manner of behavior from a theological perspective—made possible by the Christ-event and appropriated by faith in Christ. (2:12)[6]

Titus is given this exhortation in the next verse to mark the fact that self-control must saturate all areas of the young man in every area of his life

Being able to make wise decisions, hold their passions at bay, think before they act, and keep a cool head, all would be helpful for younger Christian men. Men need to be trained in these areas, because their ability to do so will make or break the church, the family, and their place in the world. The restored men, family, and the church must take responsibility to facilitate the intentional focusing of young men.

Being reasonable points to the commitment of men in peer and authoritative relationships. Reasonability is deeply connected to teachability. Now anyone who knows me knows that I have an extremely low tolerance for people who are not teachable, especially men. When people despise wisdom from others, they are a danger to themselves and others (Prov. 13:13;

15:20). Conversely, the teachable can often avoid the pitfalls of their contemporaries, for reception of wisdom preserves the prudent (Prov. 15:32). The teachable person is also peaceable because having a disposition of reasonableness aids in dissolving tension in relationships.

Maybe most of all, having one's passions under control will help young men not seek illegitimate outlets for divinely given passions. We don't need to rehash the sexual opportunities available to today's young man. It's no wonder, then, that self-control should permeate the entire being of the young man.

Instruction for Older Men (Titus 2)

I am an avid lover of older mature believers. They have such a soothing disposition because they have spent years honing their love for Jesus, the gospel, and the Word of God. The believer Paul describes in this passage is the picture of maturity, one who has stood the test of time and over that time has been molded and formed by the hand of Jesus in their lives. It's a vision of what all of us should aspire to in our future.

Sober-Minded

This is a man who is level-headed. Similar to self-control, this characteristic points to the ability to have great restraint. It also points to one who is un-intoxicated with the world. This seasoned believer can think clearly and objectively and can offer wisdom and insight to those around him.

Dignified

When I hear the word dignified, I see a man in a Harris Tweed suit with suede elbow patches, with a pair of 1,000-mile Wolverine wingtips, a vintage calfskin briefcase, gingham oxford shirt, with a paisley bow tie, duckbill Gatsby hat, and a pair of Brendel eyeglasses. That's a grown man outfit, and it speaks of dignity and prestige. That's what the word means, too—"worthy of respect and honor; noble and serious."[7] It signifies that which lifts "the mind from the cheap and tawdry to that which is noble and good and of moral worth"[8] This doesn't mean that a dignified man is above or aloof to humor and laughter. It does mean, however, that this man is above what is ordinary and is therefore worthy of special respect.[9]

Like aged wine, this man is an asset to the community. In Paul's mind, this kind of man was beyond youthful vigor, and out of all the men in the congregation, this man was to have both spiritual and natural maturity. His sheer presence made you watch your tongue as well as your manners, and in a word, grow up.

This kind of man is comfortable in his own skin. He doesn't feel the need to act younger than he actually is like some of the men in my neighborhood who insist on wearing Timberlands, Jordan's, Nike Posite, Air Force 1s, and fitted caps. To be honest, it is incredibly embarrassing. Their clothes reflect their maturity and temperament. Proverbs 20:29 gives another vision of age: "The glory of young men is their strength, and the splendor of old men is gray hair."[10] Older men are to find honor in what has been gained from walking with God over the years and being able to put on display a dignity that drives the younger to strive for that type of dignified maturity.

Self-Controlled

As it pertains to the older men, this word points to their prudence and sober-mindedness that flows from Christ and years of practiced faith in the gospel. Affections for the Lord bleed from this man. Their passions are firmly under control; they have been well settled and trained by the righteousness that comes from God through Jesus. The control of the tongue (James 3:5–9), the sexual faculties (2 Tim. 2:22), and the expressiveness of liberties (Rom. 14) aren't perfect, but they are bridled. The man finds himself in a sober place of maturity as the Lord has grown him through much suffering and mistakes.

Sound in Faith

Throughout the pastoral epistles Paul uses the term *sound* to describe spiritual health particularly in relation to doctrine or content of teaching. Here it is used in concert with the three pillars of the Christian faith: these men are called to be sound in faith, hope, and love (1 Cor. 13:13; 1 Thess. 1:3; 1 Tim. 6:11). What an honor to call the older men in the church to exalt these attributes for the people of God in a healthy way.

Of the three, they are first called to walk in a healthy or sound faith. Faith is at the core of the Christian faith because it is given by the Lord as a means to believe in Jesus and to serve Him in serving others (Rom. 12:3).

One of the greatest joys of my walk with Jesus is to have seen older believers survive heart failure, cancer, chemotherapy, high blood pressure, wayward children, marital problems, broken friendships, church hurt, and much more, and yet still walk onward with God. In their walk, they place these sufferings in a sound, biblical perspective. There is an unspoken stability sustained by faith in the gospel in these men who have been faith tested and yet grown through life. It's this kind of sound faith that motivates other men and women to place all our confidence in Jesus. These great survivors must be watched as model disciple makers as they help those younger than them in the faith.

I've heard older believers say on occasion around Epiphany Fellowship that the church is too young for them. I lovingly challenge this notion, trying to help them see that the young in our fellowship desperately need their presence. If your church is made up of primarily young people, you are missing a vital component for spiritual maturity. Seek out the older. Bring them in. Let these mature believers model what it means to walk with Jesus for years and years.

Sound in Love

These older believers must also be healthy in love. This soundness in love shows up in how these believers sacrificially love on every level. It is the gospel, deeply rooted and grown over time, that makes this sacrificial love possible. Sound and healthy love is willing to sacrifice in order to see Jesus formed in others, giving for the mission of God, and the education of children just to name a few. It is love extended to the sinner and the broken, and love that is given for the edification of the church. It is also the kind of love that can be very difficult for men.

Men need to learn how to love tenderly, love hard, and to give tough love as well as receive it. Once again, Jesus serves as our example as He loves us through rebukes, relentless presence, and ultimately a brutal death.

Sound in Steadfastness

Being healthy in steadfastness is a powerful need in our day of entitlement. Entitlement thinks it deserves what it receives, but steadfastness is instead thankful for what it receives because it teaches appreciation through challenge. Steadfastness means "the capacity to hold out or bear up in the face of difficulty, patience, endurance, fortitude, and perseverance."[11] Jesus not only gave us the example of steadfastness (1 Pet. 2:21), He empowered us through the gospel to deal with the pending suffering that comes with being in Him (Gal. 5:22–24; James 1:1–3; 2 Pet. 1:4–7). Steadfastness doesn't just hold on, but holds on in faith, believing in the loving care of Jesus at all times.

This is one characteristic in particularly short supply in the men of today. We see that shortness in the abandonment of women and children. Men must begin to be characterized by gospel-driven steadfastness. Then, when challenges come, men remain and bear the majority of the burden for their homes.

On *Good Times*, one of my favorite sitcoms, James Evans's father wanted to return for a visit though James hadn't seen him in thirty years. As he struggled through the episode, he finally confronted his father for his reckless abandonment of the family. At the confrontation, his father responded like this: "Son, things were hard and I figured that me leaving would have meant one less mouth to feed."

What a coward. This was a picture of a man not only refusing to own up to his responsibility, but then attempting to make his actions seem sacrificial and heroic. Let me say it clearly, men: Abandonment—and that's precisely what it is—is never a solution. It never takes away pain, but only adds to it.

Though women are, most of the time, seen in the home as those with the most commitment and fortitude, the Lord wants older men to rise up as examples of endurance. My father was a Buffalo Soldier in WWII and the Korean War. He talks about the extreme circumstances that they had to endure, going so far as hiding among dead bodies to evade the enemy. On another occasion, when the enemy was bombing them, they would lay in bomb craters because the likelihood of bombs falling in the same place was slim. He and the other soldiers would pray to the Lord and ask Him to give them the steadfastness to make it home. When they returned, he received two Purple Hearts for being shot in the wars and yet was still called the N-word upon returning to the States. The mental pain that it caused him was unimaginable, and yet he endured. He was steadfast. That's what we must return to. That's what we need.

The Blessing of Children

Nowhere in the Bible is vision for the family cast more compellingly than in Psalms 127 and 128. Whenever I feel overwhelmed and unclear as a leader and lover of my family, I take a visit to these psalms. They aid in re-rooting us in God's passion for men to know where we are going as leaders of the family.

These passages give a glorious overview of what it looks like to be a family, specifically in the area of raising children. Both have a masculine overtone, and men are instructed as to how we center our homes on the Lord and His divine focus for them. In both psalms there are two massive concepts that dictate the potency of the vision cast in each to men for family: The Lord as the builder of the house, and the fear of the Lord. Both are intimately connected in the life of a man as the home is being developed.

My youngest son is at the end of the toddler stage of development. I enjoy watching him play and explore, whether he's playing the drums, singing at the top of his lungs, or riding his scooter. It's only when he starts playing with Legos that I get a little concerned. When he builds, he does so in a way that the blocks are going to fall apart. Everything is slapped together without concern for stability. His foundation is usually built with the smaller blocks instead of the larger ones, and he doesn't yet know to spread the foundation wide enough to support the height of the structure he wants to create. But when I step in and try and fix the stability problems, he makes sure everyone in the neighborhood knows that it's his building—not mine. So he builds on, only to have the frustration of seeing what he built come tumbling down.

Old habits die hard. As men we tend to build our lives and homes in a similar fashion. God is standing close by wanting to help us build stability into our homes, but we keep pushing His hands away, determined to do it the way we want to. The ability to allow the Lord to build for us flows from our fear of Him. Fearing the Lord means standing in awe of the reality of who God is. When we fear the Lord, we live our lives knowing that God is watching. God in Christ has restored our vision for this—for the believer, fearing God isn't a terror; it's a pleasure. Because Jesus has removed all condemnation, we no longer see the Lord as judge. We can instead stand in awe of His nature and trust in His immense strength on our behalf.

God will strengthen the homes of the fathers who fear and trust in Him. We are not passive participants in this strengthening, standing idly by and waiting for God to somehow move. We are active in obedience, all the while recognizing that the strength comes from resting in the Lord to do the work we can't do. We recognize that our labor is in vain if the Lord isn't empowering our vigor. Woe to the man who thinks his pursuits can have value without the presence of God. But, as we see in Psalm 128, when we fear the Lord, we enjoy the Lord and what He has provided (v. 2). Nothing on Earth is like working and knowing that the Lord is being pleased. It is blessing without regret. That's what children are supposed to be—blessing without regret.

Compare that, though, to the situation we find ourselves in now, when children are merely the unintended consequence of premarital sex. Whether in the inner city or the suburbs, very few people today see children in the same way the Bible pictures them, as a heritage or a gift from the Lord. Translated into our cultural opinion, we might say children are a challenge at best or a gag gift from heaven at worst:

"Ha ha ha . . . funny, God."

More than a decade ago, my wife had a third trimester miscarriage. It was devastating to us. We were broken and hurt by experiencing the loss of our first child. As time went on we were told by doctors that she probably wouldn't have any children. When we finally had a baby, our appreciation was different because the Lord used that tragedy to create in us a greater appreciation for children and life. Circumstantially He helped us to develop His heart for what children represent. God willing, it won't have to happen like that for you. By His grace, we can begin to have a restored vision for what children really are.

Giving Them Restored Focus

Heaven views children as a gift that needs to be directed. They are "Like arrows in the hand of a warrior" (Ps. 127:4). I love this verbal picture:

> Archery units were the most critical component of an ancient army—useful on foot, on horseback, and as part of the chariot corp (Yadin, *The Art of Warfare*, 6–8, 295–26). The psalmist's choice of arrows as a metaphor is appropriate to the analogy of multiple children, but it also underscores that the growth of

the next generation is vital to the future well-being of both city and society.[12]

Some prefer to translate this term with the gender neutral "children," but "sons" are plainly in view here, as the following verses make clear. Daughters are certainly wonderful additions to a family, but in ancient Israelite culture sons were the "arrows" that gave a man security in his old age, for they could defend the family interests at the city gate, where the legal and economic issues of the community were settled.[13]

Sons are to be given direction by their fathers on how to lead a household. This is necessary when you start to see your sons as future leaders of homes. When we see our boys like this, the metaphor makes even more sense. We direct our sons, as an archer directs his arrows, to the interests of the Lord. Archers don't aimlessly point the tip of their arrow; they spend great time and care in order to master hitting a target. Young men hunger for their dads to lead them. Spending time with our sons is unforgettable for them. In that time, we might show them all kinds of things about what it means to be a man, but the most important target we can point them to is Jesus (Heb. 12:1–3). It's not only teaching them to be strong; it's not only teaching them to be self-controlled. Pointing them toward gospel targets aid them in having a sharpened view of where they are to go and what to shoot for in life.

One time I was extremely angry with my oldest son. I don't remember what he did, but I know that my anger meter was high. I brought him into his room where he no doubt thought that he would get a spanking. Instead, I took the belt and explained the gospel to him. I explained how God took out His anger on Jesus instead of us. As he prepared himself for the spanking he was sure would come, I began to hit myself with the belt. I told him that I was taking the beating for him just as Jesus did on the cross. Suddenly the whole thing clicked for him. He saw the gospel. He understood that Jesus was his substitute. And he will never forget that. As fathers, we have to create memories that have deep and systemic biblical lessons attached to them. Nowadays, I take my oldest son with me sometimes when I travel. I use it as father/son teaching moments as he gets to see new cities, churches, and enjoy plane flights. It has been extremely fruitful for pointing him to Jesus.

Arrows were also used to defend against enemies. In the day of the psalmist, growing children would help a father unable to defend and protect the household at the same level in old age. Fathers would work hard to train sons to protect the interest of the family in the city in which they dwelled. Not only that, but they would defend the interests of the Lord:

> Arrows are used in combat to defend oneself against enemies; sons are viewed here as providing social security and protection (see v. 5). The phrase "sons of youth" is elliptical, meaning "sons [born during the father's] youth." Such sons will have grown up to be mature adults and will have children of their own by the time the father reaches old age and becomes vulnerable to enemies. Contrast the phrase "son of

old age" in Gen. 37:3 (see also 44:20), which refers to Jacob's age when Joseph was born.[14]

In Solomon's day grown children normally cared for their parents in their old age. They would defend them as the parents became increasingly dependent and vulnerable. That is what Solomon evidently had in mind in verses 4 and 5. Children (sons) can be a defense for their parents from exterior and interior foes. Arrows defend against attacking invaders. Negotiating in the gate pictures defending against enemies who would seek to rob the defenseless through legal maneuvering and bring shame on them. Thus children can be a kind of insurance policy but not one that someone can work hard to buy. They are a gift from God.[15]

It fills me with hope and joy to think of my sons having a masculine passion to defend the honor of the Lord and His desires. Sons are the warriors that are developed. The Scripture has much to say about the impact and possibilities of the Word in the life of young men. To see this come to fruition, we must be active in teaching them the following:

- Not to be ashamed of the gospel (Rom. 1:16)
- The word of God matures you beyond your years (Ps. 119:99)
- Have courage in the midst of great challenge (Josh. 1:8–10)
- Stand up when others want to bow (Dan. 3)
- Youth is not an excuse for immaturity (1 Tim. 4:12)

This is God's vision for the home. Men have the immense pleasure and responsibility of involving themselves in His work. We must—MUST—be active participants in the lives of all our children, but especially our sons.

CHAPTER 8

Restored Church

 Boyz in the Hood is a classic movie that depicts the challenges and difficulties of growing up in an urban context. One scene particularly memorable to me takes place on the porch of a character named Dough Boy. The subject matter is women. Chris, one of the other main characters, states things plainly: "I know where you can find a lot of fine women—church." Seems pretty random, but the truth is that many people see church in this light. Church is a place filled with women.

We have all heard the stats about men's general disinterest in church. The ratio of women to men is not merely a general population issue; it's an engagement issue. The church of God must focus in on manhood as an essential to discipleship. The church must take on an active role in restoring the image of men through Jesus. We must work hard at engaging men beyond breakfasts and small events. There must be a concerted effort to make sure that the church is where manhood can be seen and trained.

My sons always ask me to draw their favorite characters from cartoons for them. As I am drawing, many times they begin to say, "Daddy, that isn't the way he looks." I tell them that I am doing the best I can to portray what they are asking me to draw. However, it tends to fall short often. The same is true when it comes to our portrayal of manhood and connecting with men.

Jesus' death on the cross created a new manhood (Eph. 2:15). Though this passage is about mankind in general, it includes the restoration of God's intention for the individual genders. In Christ, then, men are being restored into true men. The church is the only place in the world empowered to show forth this new manhood. Because the church is God's restored community, it has been laced with the nutrients to give eternal snapshots of God's image to the world. God's manifold wisdom can and is only seen through the church (Eph. 3:10). The church, in other words, is the HD version of reality. It has been appointed to the high call of giving a vivid image of God's intention for the world. Robust masculinity is not a macho goofball; it's an eternally ingenious reflection of the God-Man.

How, then, can the church be reclaimed as a place that embraces true masculinity? That's where we turn next.

Defeminizing the Church

Riskianity

For many years, Jesus has been seen (both literally and figuratively) as an effeminate man. Many portraits of Jesus in the church (if they are even supposed to be there) are of a weak Clark Kentish, mild-mannered, soft man. We must be careful in the church to communicate that the same meek and lowly Jesus who humbled Himself to the will of His Father was also the temple cleanser on a rampage for His Father's glory. We have erred too often for the former to the neglect of the latter, presenting a Jesus that women relate to most closely. David Murrow says it best:

> A business guru once said, "Your system is perfectly designed to give you the results you're getting." Christianity's primary delivery system, the local church, is perfectly designed to reach women and older folks. That's why our pews are filled with them. But this church system offers little to stir the masculine heart, so men find it dull and irrelevant. The more masculine the man, the more likely he is to dislike church.
>
> What do I mean? Men and young adults are drawn to risk, challenge and adventure. But these things are discouraged in the local church. Instead, most congregations offer a safe, nurturing community—an oasis of stability and predictability. Studies show that women and seniors gravitate toward these things. Although our official mission is one of adventure, the actual mission of most congregations is making people feel comfortable and safe—especially longtime members.
>
> How did Christianity, founded by a man and his 12 male disciples, become the province of women? There

is a pattern of feminization in Christianity going back at least 700 years, according to Dr. Leon Podles, author of *The Church Impotent: The Feminization of Christianity*. But the ball really got rolling in the 1800s. With the dawning of the Industrial Revolution, large numbers of men sought work in mines, mills and factories, far from home and familiar parish. Women stayed behind, and began remaking the church in their image. The Victorian era saw the rise of church nurseries, Sunday schools, lay choirs, quilting circles, ladies' teas, soup kitchens, girls' societies, potluck dinners, etc.

Soon, the very definition of a good Christian had changed: boldness and aggression were out; passivity and receptivity were in. Christians were to be gentle, sensitive and nurturing, focused on home and family rather than accomplishment and career. Believers were not supposed to like sex, tobacco, dancing or other worldly pleasures. The godly were always calm, polite and sociable. This feminine spirituality still dominates our churches. Those of us who grew up in church hardly notice it; we can't imagine things any other way. But a male visitor detects the feminine spirit the moment he walks in the sanctuary door. He may feel like Tom Sawyer in Aunt Polly's parlor; he must watch his language, mind his manners and be extra polite. It's hard for a man to be real in church because he must squeeze himself into this feminine religious mold.[1]

This cannot be stated any better. The riskless environment creates boredom. While we shouldn't negate the importance of nurturing and safety, we need churches that present men with God-sized visions that make their hearts sink like they were on the steepest roller coaster on the planet. Initiatives like church planting, pioneering missions, and missional engagement of men in the city inspire and challenge the intrinsic part of men who love to be challenged. Getting on mission with Jesus is quite the journey. What else would make twelve manly men drop their former lives and become fishers of men? Compelling, risky, Jesus-centered, gospel-driven vision rendering divine results is the secret sauce of changing men's attitude toward church. Men want to be a part of something that matters.

We see this so richly in the Bible. Before Paul met Jesus, he was focused and driven by what he thought was pleasing to God: persecuting the church (Acts 7:51–8:1). But after Jesus knocked him down on the Damascus Road, Paul pursued an even riskier calling:

> "Lord," Ananias answered, "I have heard from many people about this man, how much harm he has done to Your saints in Jerusalem. And he has authority here from the chief priests to arrest all who call on Your name." But the Lord said to him, "Go! For this man is My chosen instrument to take My name to Gentiles, kings, and the Israelites. I will show him how much he must suffer for My name!" (Acts 9:13–16)

Paul was called to travel, raise money, plant churches, be shipwrecked, beaten, see visions of heaven, preach the gospel where it hadn't been preached, disciple men, develop leaders, go to territories where Jews were hated, to kings who could kill him, and to be chased by thieves. There is nothing effeminate about following Jesus. That's what men need to see. Being in Jesus and living for the gospel is the greatest voyage a man can be a part of in life. To join the living God as an apprentice in His effort to reveal His kingdom is the most fulfilling and exciting life imaginable. To those who want to go all in with Jesus, He gives kingdom rank (1 Pet. 2:9) and personal rewards upon entry into heaven (Matt. 25:23). This kind of vision will capture the hearts and passions of men. But that's not all we must capture.

Intellectual Engagement

Men's minds must also be challenged. As an unbeliever, I was a Black Nationalist, believing Christianity to be the white man's religion of anti-intellectualism. I did not consider "thinking" to be of any consequence for the Christian; instead, I saw Christianity as intellectually anemic and overemotional. Sermons seemed overly simplistic, historically disconnected, theologically thin, and unattached to real life. When I engaged in discussion with believers, my thoughts were confirmed as many of them were not intellectually equipped to deal with those who did not believe in the historic Christian faith.

When God saved me, 1 Peter 3:15 became incredibly meaningful to me. It showed me that Christianity must engage the mind as well as the heart: "Always be ready to give a defense to anyone who asks you for a reason for the hope that is in you."

When I read the Gospel accounts of life of Jesus, I saw the Lord fearlessly engaging every question brought to Him. He faced His opponents with intellectual prowess and strength. The more I read about Him the more I wanted to be like Him. I found strength in His self-confidence and was driven to communicate who He is in like fashion.

In studying the Bible further I found even more that it had to say concerning the mind. The gospel will renew our minds to think better for God (Ezek. 36:25–27; Rom. 12:1–2). This renewal is necessary in order for us to be truly loyal. In renewing our minds, the Lord is creating followers who don't only think about the truth, but walk in light of the truth. Indeed, part of our eternal destiny is wound up in knowing more and more of God.

This knowledge of God is only attainable through the new mind (1 Cor. 2:16). Thomas Watson said it best in *The Godly Man's Picture:*

A godly man shows his love to the Written Word:

By diligently READING it. The noble Bereans "searched the Scriptures daily" (Acts 17:11). Apollos was mighty in the Scriptures (Acts 18:24). The Word is our Magna Charta for heaven; we should be daily reading over this charter. The Word shows what is truth, and what is error. It is the field where the pearl of great price is hidden. How we should dig for this pearl! A godly man's heart is the library to hold the

Word of God; it dwells richly in him (Col. 3:16). It is reported of Melanchthon that when he was young, he always carried the Bible with him and read it greedily. The Word has a double work: to *teach* us and to *judge* us. Those who will not be taught by the Word, shall be judged by the Word. Oh, let us make ourselves familiar with the Scripture! What if it should be as in the times of Diocletian, who commanded by proclamation that the Bible be burned? Or as in Queen Mary's days, when it spelled death to have a Bible in English? *By diligent conversing with Scripture, we may carry a Bible in our heads!*[2]

The Word of life is a sufficient treasury to satisfy the latent intellect of the new mind of men. We are to mine it for all it is worth. The narratives in the historical books are more than enough to rival any Hollywood blockbuster. We must unfold these stories with men in mind. One of the greatest narrative preachers of our generation is the late Bishop Gilbert Earl Patterson, pastor of the Temple Church of God in Christ in Memphis, Tennessee. His sermons are legendary as being mainly from the historical books. His ability to tell the redemptive-historical picture in a masculine and Christ-centered way has challenged many a man. He knew his Bible well. I remember him describing David fighting a battle and it was told in a way that was exegetically accurate, theologically rich, intellectually stimulating, and with masculine connection.

Dr. Tony Evans was the first pastor that proved to me that men could have intellectual prowess through Jesus.

It wasn't just his ThM or ThD from Dallas Theological Seminary, but how he used that education to intellectually engage men. Consequently, when I looked around Oak Cliff Bible Fellowship, the church where Dr. Evans pastors, it was almost 50 percent men led by a community of intellectually engaged male elders. The visibly masculine male presence in the church called me up. These men were lovers of the Word and were committed to biblical Christianity. When we engage the minds of men, showing them that Christianity is indeed for those who think, Jesus is lifted up and men are inspired to follow Him.

Adding Masculinity to Worship Gatherings

There are some more practical ways to make sure that our churches are appealing to men. But most Christians don't realize how male unfriendly the church is. Let me give a few suggestions about how our gatherings for worship might become places that welcome and appeal to men.

Making the Church Facility Masculine

It was launch Sunday at Epiphany Fellowship. We were taking the ministry of this local urban church public. I had searched our neighborhood for facilities for quite some time before securing a building for our worship space, men's and women's groups, and outreach events. There was only one problem: the facility was filled with pastel colors. I knew men would cringe at the pink hallways and the sea green basement. It would be a deep inhibition for the men to feel at home in this environment. It's not that God can't move in such an environment; He can and did in our case. The point is that we must make the effort—if we want to recruit men to the cause of Jesus—to make sure our buildings are masculinely flavored. To this day, I don't allow a bunch of flowers or plants around the pulpit where I preach. It's not because I don't like greenery; it's because we are vitally concerned that the church is welcoming to men.

Masculine Musicians

Effeminate musicians might be the most visible means by which men are turned off to the church. Perhaps you're thinking this is a little nit-picky on my part, but I would maintain that a man, when leading worship, has the power to distract with his worship expression, conversation, mannerisms, and even dress. It is a pink elephant many times that the church won't deal with. I am not in any way homophobic and pressing us to treat people who have and do struggle with the sin of immorality in the form of homosexuality by denying them the blessings that come with forgiveness through Jesus. However, it is important we recognize who and what we are placing before God's people in leadership of the worship gathering. In that recognition, we must consider whether we are encouraging or distracting those present. When men like this are present in dominant and public form, it could send the wrong message to men about the church. There is some practical instruction in 1 Corinthians 11:4 that can help us here: "Every man who prays or prophesies with something on his head dishonors his head."

The men in this context were not to distract the public gathering of the saints by wearing a head covering that signified their social status in the local church. Jesus is to be supremely exalted in the gathering of the saints; men's purpose in leadership is to point to Him, not signify social status and preference. The overall principle from this verse is that we should remove everything in the worship gathering that is a distraction to the gospel, exaltation of Jesus, and edification of the body. These distractions can come in the form of attire, speech, and any other chronic anthropocentricism. I cannot tell you how many times I have heard men complain about this issue. We must work to remove all obstacles to the gospel in our gatherings.

This is one way we value all those who walk through the doors of the church building. When we think through issues like this, we do so making sure that these simple decisions are motivated by whether or not we can further the mission of God in the world. These decisions aren't made based on form, but function.

The church must have men in leadership who express themselves in a godly and manly way. First Timothy 2:8 states: "Therefore, I want the men in every place to pray, lifting up holy hands without anger or argument." Men are called to lead the church in pure worship when it gathers. This doesn't mean that the worship leaders (for our context) need to be men, but that the men present dominate in voice and expression. Whether in song or simultaneous prayer and worship, men are to be expressions of God's divine order in worship gatherings.[3]

In this way, men can restore order and peace in worship gatherings through their leadership:

> But the present passage also reveals that the anger and arguments of some men were contributing to the disruption of the church's worship service. As pointed out above (see on 2:1), Paul drew upon certain material in such cases in order to restore peace to the community by encouraging appropriate behavior. In this his concern both for biblical patterns and for the perceptions of those outside of the church is evident.[4]

Nothing against the sisters, but there is nothing like the sound of men in the gathering of the saints, worshipping the Lord with broken hearts. The local Christian church should have an unparalleled male presence in its midst. Since God is the originator of manhood and Jesus Christ is the restorer of it, His redeemed community must have the choicest of men to exemplify His eternal reign.

Masculine Songs

Yep. The songs matter too. Much of what we sing is a little weird for men to be driven to worship. I have at times cringed as I've looked around at men during songs. We tend to think men are unspiritual because they sometimes don't participate in musical worship, but maybe their disengagement is connected to the overwhelming content of songs, culture of worship expression, and musical mood.

We don't have to fully accommodate men when it comes to song content, but we do need to think of them when we make song selections. For men who have grown up in the church, it is something we have gotten used to and make room for, but for those new to the faith at an older age (teen+), the transition can be a little rough. Do we really think singing things like "hold me," "rock me in your arms," "you are beautiful," and "you are so sweet" appeals to men? Our insistence on these kinds of songs points to the ongoing over-feminizing of the church.

We can utilize the principles of expressions like God being beautiful, but communicate them in ways that are man friendly. In Psalm 27:4, David writes,

> I have asked one thing from the LORD; it is what I desire: to dwell in the house of the LORD all the days of my life, gazing on the beauty of the LORD and seeking Him in His temple.

The word for *beauty* means splendor and delightful. The point is that the psalmist admires the attributes of the Lord and is stating that they are exciting to look at and meditate upon.

> He would be able "to gaze upon the beauty of the Lord," not to be interpreted literally, but as implying the extraordinary experience of God's beauty and glory as symbolized in the temple, specifically in the Ark.[5]

As the worshipper was in the temple he would have been drawn to the attributes of God by the objects and people in the temple who exemplified them in the various expressions of worship. The extractable principle for us today isn't so much saying that God is beautiful, though He is, but making sure the environment is set to draw us into worship. A man looking at a Bugatti, Maybach Benz, or a Bentley can enjoy looking at it. He would then offer a viable appraisal of its appearance that would make sense to those around him.

In the gathering of the saints, we must push each other onward to live increasingly effective lives for Jesus: And let us consider how to stir up one another to love and good works (Heb. 10:24 ESV). The word for "stir up" is a tense one. It means to provoke, make angry, or to set something on fire. What a great use of language for men. We need to be set ablaze for Jesus in our gatherings. This is what helps God's people not want to forsake the gathering of one another together. Christian men should not have to drag each other to gatherings; they should be set ablaze by the God of heaven so much that they are the first ones in the door, leading their families behind them.

The same David who reflected on the beauty of the Lord knew what it means to be set ablaze by his worship. That fire inside him is what motivated him to stand in the face of insurmountable odds and face down a giant twice his size. Because he was a worshipper, David's vision of God was much larger than the giant:

> "Your servant has been tending his father's sheep. Whenever a lion or a bear came and carried off a lamb from the flock, I went after it, struck it down, and rescued the lamb from its mouth. If it reared up against

me, I would grab it by its fur, strike it down, and kill it. Your servant has killed lions and bears; this uncircumcised Philistine will be like one of them, for he has defied the armies of the living God." Then David said, "The LORD who rescued me from the paw of the lion and the paw of the bear will rescue me from the hand of this Philistine." Saul said to David, "Go, and may the LORD be with you." (1 Sam. 17:34–37)

When men are inspired in worship, they have the courage to face the greatest of ills.

Godly Pastors

The role of pastors in the church is to lead, feed, know, care, protect, and project. As leaders, pastors must guide God's people into God's visionary directives for their lives (1 Tim. 5:17), communicate the truth of God's Word in a sound way (Titus 3:1), know deeply the people entrusted with them, care about their brokenness, and protect the people of God against false teaching and divisiveness among them (Titus 1; 3:9–10).

Pastors must exemplify the kind of character I have advocated for throughout this book. They are not only an example to the flock overall, but especially the men among them. These should be the quintessential men who can lead others into manhood. They are the men from whom men learn how to be men. They must lead their men in the development of a rich culture of manhood in the church that strips away macho self-righteousness while at the same time encourages true and manly strength and confidence.

Restoring Spiritual Authority

There are two extremes in the church when it comes to spiritual authority: pastor worship or congregational insubordination. Because of pastoral spiritual abuse, entrepreneurialism, and individualism, many have viewed spiritual authority as optional. There has been an authoritative egalitarianism that has caused many to hold no leader in the church in high regard. Pastoral abuse has only heightened the overall questioning of authority, which hip-hop culture aided in developing in the late '80s and early '90s.

On the other hand, we see many church pastors whose authority borders on worship. I've seen a television preacher speaking while one of the ministers started shining his shoes! Both extremes are destructive. We must gain a right understanding of biblical spiritual authority.

Saul's disobedience to the Lord in 1 Samuel 15:23 was likened to witchcraft. God takes seriously insubordination, defiance toward authority, or the breaking of spiritual ranks among His people. In Titus 1:9, Paul speaks of men in the church at Crete who walked in such a manner. Godly men in the church submit to godly authority. Men who posture themselves as having more insight into God's truth and are therefore incapable of submitting to leadership must be challenged (1 Tim. 1:3) or disciplined (3 John 7). Men who want to grow as men and be promoters of harmony in the church must act as a model of submissiveness and service to the leadership that the Lord has set up (Heb. 13:7).

We need organized men walking in beastly spiritual authority in the church. Men outside the church should be drawn to Jesus because of gospel-driven submission in the church to spiritual authority that exalts the God of the restored.

Spiritually Fathering Our Men and Boys

In the African-American church tradition, one of the most endearing and empowering relationships is that of the spiritual father. Ministers that received their calling to ministry under the leadership and guidance of a particular senior pastor are called "sons" of that church. In essence, those men view themselves as the ministry offspring of that particular pastor's ministry. It's a lifelong connection that we need to regain as younger men are raised up into the life of the church.

A spiritual father is one who has taken a special interest in investing in another man for the purpose of helping him look more like Jesus Christ. Theologically this flows from the fatherhood of God and the life of Jesus Christ. We have discussed this in great detail. The fatherly description of God in many facets in the Bible makes being a spiritual father rooted in God's nature as shown in His Word. God the Father loves to take up a place in the lives of those that need a deeper sense of fathering in their lives. In Psalm 27:10, "Even if my father and mother abandon me, the LORD cares for me."

When some of His people are not fathered, God will enter into a deeper sense of intimacy with them by caring for them in places where they have been abandoned by their earthly parents. Likewise, there are others who play this role in the Bible. Some are explicit and others are implicit. Jesus spiritually fathered the disciples. He built them into godly men by spending time with them up close. Paul was a spiritual father to the Corinthians (2 Cor. 1:2–3), the Thessalonians (1 Thess. 2:11), and to Timothy (1 Cor. 4:17; 1 Tim. 1:2; 2 Tim. 1:2; 2:1), and Titus (Titus 1:4). With these entries we see that these relationships were based on leading people to Jesus and walking closely with them in discipleship, in development for gospel mission, and finally in small numbers. They provide an example for older believers in the church as they seek to father other believers.

But just because a person is advanced in years doesn't mean that they are qualified to make disciples. Some older people need to be told when they are toxic, bitter, needy, divisive, hurtful, and pushy. On the other hand, we need to encourage saints who have the spiritual fortitude to make their lives available to the next generation.

Complaining about the state of a generation will not change it; investing in it will. In our own young church where the average age is twenty-five years, my challenge to seasoned believers is not to sit back and relax in their later years. Instead, they can give their lives by sewing the gospel into the lives of young people. Our churches have a deep need for this kind of intergenerational partnership. Spiritual parenting is one of the most fruitful forms of intergenerational partnership. This intentional investment includes several aspects.

Walking Closely in Discipleship

Making disciples is that mandate for all who believe, yet this needs to be amped up and connected to spiritual parenting. Men living on mission will naturally come in contact

with nonbelievers and lead them to Christ. We must emphasize the need to continue to walk alongside them as they
come into Christ and the life of the church. Paul modeled
this desire to see converts developed to the point of spiritual
stability. In 1 Thessalonians 2:11 he speaks of his fatherly
commitment to them. He "exhorted" them as a father might
do to a son. To *exhort* is to "urge strongly, appeal to, encourage, or to come alongside."[6] Spiritual fathers must know
where their sons are and come alongside of them to help
them to grow. But Paul was only modeling what he learned
from Jesus:

> Jesus modeled spiritual fathering. Though He min-
> istered to multitudes, He spent most of His time on
> earth as a spiritual father to twelve men. He knew
> that kingdom values were caught more than taught.
> He trained them so they could grow up spiritually and
> be equipped to train others. He fished, prayed, wept,
> and rejoiced with these disciples, and they went on to
> "father" many more people in the kingdom of God.[7]

One of my spiritual sons was in need of deep development
in the area of becoming a more organized and focused leader.
I took him under my wing for eighteen months and walked
with him point by point as I watched him make mistakes. We
connected both relationally and ministerially. We had many
hard conversations and exhortations, and now God has graced
him to flourish.

Along with exhorting others, we encourage them, just
as Paul did, when we walk alongside others. Encouragement

is an expression of love. Together with participation in the Spirit and heartfelt sympathy, it forms one of the foundations of church life as lived out in the sphere of Christ (Phil. 2:1).[8] Sometimes spiritual fathers must just be there to cheer up a spiritual son in failure, loss, hurt, or identity issues. Fathering takes some level of nurturing through the difficulties of life. Paul gave the Thessalonians consolation through the suffering that they were experiencing. This consolation helped them to grow and develop as well as hold on in difficulty.

When I went through a difficult time with suffering, I connected with my spiritual father and he shepherded me through some very dark times in ministry. When I lost my daughter, he, by the aid of the Holy Spirit, helped me to shepherd my wife through this very hard time. To this day I am thankful for the relationship that the Lord has given us.

Paul also, as a spiritual father, charged his sons with walking in a manner worthy of God. To charge is to make an emphatic demand; "it is to implore and insist."[9] Spiritual fathers must call their sons to account for all that has been invested in them. Timothy would have felt it in 2 Timothy 4. Men need to feel the weight of the spiritual responsibility and investment that God has given them through spiritual parenting. But there are several ways in which spiritual parenting can go wrong, all of which must be guarded against.

Drawing people to yourself. Spiritual parenting can easily lead to pride. Spiritual sons must not be used as outlets for your own personal insecurities. Insecure people tend to develop unhealthy attachments that stunt the growth of those around them. Recognize that fathering someone shouldn't be the center of your value; Jesus should. Be aware of this tendency.

Pitfalls to Avoid

Creating overdependence. In training anyone, you want to develop in them a need to mature. No parent wants the "Lamont Sanford Syndrome"—a son who stays at home forever. We must push men to a dependent-independence: dependence on Jesus and an independence of others (unless others are necessary). Spiritual fathers must be a resource, not an enabler.

Guilt-driven spirituality. Legalism and fear of man should never be the motivation for growth. Neither fear nor guilt should be the main motivation. The gospel must be. Men love being challenged but not manipulated by guilt. Loyalty comes through love.

Overbearing. Just because men aren't "weaker vessels" doesn't mean they don't have weaknesses. Some well-meaning men can use their influence to be too overbearing and abrasive. There are appropriate times for strong and firm speech, but that must not be the relational standard.

Ministering outside the realm of spiritual authority. Spiritual fathering must not be used as a means to override the existing spiritual authority in the church, but complement it. Encouraging men to be under authority is important. Being an outlet for rebellion isn't healthy.

Acting like people belong to you. Spiritual children belong to God—not you. Be careful of treating them like they are your personal possession.

Goals to Restoring Manhood

Encourage their ability to live out God's truth. In 2 Timothy, Paul knows that he is about to die and that Timothy will have to live in light of what and how Paul has fathered him. As he challenges him, he also encourages him in the Word of God. He assumes, based on the power of the gospel, that he is able to live out what he is telling him. This type of confidence encourages sons. I can remember the encouragement of my elders and how they blessed me by confidently affirming my ability and commitment to the Scriptures.

Empower them to be leaders in their sphere. This is huge! All men have been called by God to lead on some level, especially if they have a family. Release them to lead. Show them that Christ has placed this ability in them and affirm them in that. Show them how to take the initiative for the benefit of others. Let them know that leading is a sacrifice. Doing so will be a part of their journey forever.

Push them to grow beyond you. Growing beyond you is a must. You are limited in what you have to offer them, but Jesus isn't. Push them hard in this direction. Let them know that they must be in a place of lifetime equipping for Jesus. Paul told Timothy "to take pains" in his growth. That type of encouragement and coaching helps the spiritual athlete to hear your voice in their soul for the rest of their lives.

Encourage them in their gifts. There is nothing like someone you look up to seeing what God has placed in you and encouraging you to live in light of it. Paul tells Timothy to "stir up the gift" (2 Tim. 1:6 KJV) and "do not neglect the gift" (1 Tim. 4:14). Inferentially, Paul is affirming Timothy's abilities and

God's investment in him. Spiritual fathers must privately and publicly do the same.

Overall, the church must take seriously the engagement of men. I am hopeful we will. I pray that as the church grows, so does the influence of men inside it. But this won't come by accident. We, in the church, must take on an intentionally deeper commitment in engaging men. With such a global crisis in manhood, how can we neglect so great a need? We must not make this a mere auxiliary or relegate it to a ministry area, but make male engagement a priority of the church at large.

Rise up, men. The world is waiting.

Conclusion

 The more I grow as a disciple of Jesus, not to mention a husband, father, and pastor, the more deeply I am convinced of the systemic need in our culture for men to be explicitly and intentionally engaged by the Word of God and the gospel. The Bible both generally and specifically recognizes the fact that discipleship of different genders and ages will look differently. That is why these differences need to be taken into careful consideration as we build structures around the way each is executed. The Pastoral Epistles and Proverbs, in particular, aid us in recognizing these distinctions.

Although most of the Bible takes on a masculine overtone, there are gender specific exhortations in several texts, specific in their context and application. In 1 Peter 3, for instance, the apostle Peter exhorts husbands and wives differently as to how they should remain faithful to Jesus in marriage in the midst of suffering. In Titus 2, Paul commands Titus to teach what accords with sound doctrine. Upon viewing the accompanying verses, though, we see that age and gender are to be tackled in different ways when it comes to recognizing how each one grows in looking more like Jesus.

In light of this understanding of discipleship distinction, we must take seriously the need for the development of manhood in particular in our lives, homes, churches, and cities. It is not enough to generally teach about discipleship; we must make distinct and specialized effort toward the growth of men. I was speaking to a friend who pastors a fairly large church about this subject and he asked me, "Emase, do you think that all churches should be making a concerted effort to have a ministry to disciple men? I mean our small groups cover the lion's share of our discipleship." My statement in response was simple: "Whether you make it formal or informal, pastors must take seriously and lead the charge in discipling men." A pastor must not only be involved in personally executing these relationships; he must set the tone for the men of the church to see this as a biblical priority.

We cannot leave the functional leading of God's people to chance. If we don't take the initiative, the adversary gladly will, just as he has in the past. Nowhere in the biblical record do we find genocide to be gender-specific to women. There was genocide of nations, but when it came to God's people, the devil always attacked the seed of the woman—the man. From Adam, to Moses, to the Lord Jesus, Satan knows that systemic change comes from men taking their proper place under the authority of Christ. I don't mean to demean the glorious place of women; I do, however, feel a great need and urgency to bring light to a great need in our culture. I have received much criticism from those who think that I am too "man-conscious," but I live in a city bereft of men willing and able to lead, love, and serve.

My hope is that this book acts not only as a wake-up call and catalyst for men to take a hard look at their own lives, but that it would also become a tool for fathers to shepherd their boys into gospel-driven men. I want to see fatherless men come to understand what was missing from their own lives and recognize God's sufficient ability to fill that gap. I long for women to see what a biblical man looks like and for marriages across our land to be transformed. I want to see pastors using this tool to spark a movement of men discipling men in their cities. I long to see men, by their very lives, dispel the myths about Jesus, the gospel, and Christian manhood, and demonstrate that manhood to the lost.

In the gospel, Jesus is restoring our vision of manhood. He is blowing up our own versions of what it means to be a man with His own quintessential masculinity. His life, death, love, and resurrection push us onward to our restored relationship with God and others. Hopefully, all the biblical evidence, exegetical notes, and practical pictorials found in this book have served the purpose, above all else, of pointing us again and again to Jesus as the great restorer of manhood.

In Him and in Him alone, we can find that the gospel is applied to all areas of our lives that we might become the men God intended for us to be—those conformed to the image of Jesus Christ. Let us, then, commit our lives to journeying with our Savior, having repented and being restored by grace alone through faith alone in Jesus Christ alone.

NOTES

Chapter 1

1. NET notes in *NET Bible First Edition* (Biblical Studies Press, 2006), http://net.bible.org.

2. J. Swanson, *Dictionary of Biblical Languages with Semantic Domains: Hebrew Old Testament* (Oak Harbor: Logos Research Systems, Inc., 1997, electronic edition).

3. NET Notes in *NET Bible*, http://net.bible.org.

4. Ibid.

5. W. A. Grudem, *Biblical Foundations for Manhood and Womanhood* (Wheaton, IL: Crossway Books, 2002), 78.

6. A *vice-regent* is a person who acts in the name of another.

7. NET Notes in *NET Bible*, http://net.bible.org.

8. Ibid.

9. The language found in this passage is known as "anthropomorphism." It's the assignment of human characteristics to God as a way of understanding the divine. It does not literally mean that God was sorry, for to say so would imply that God made a mistake. Rather, it speaks to the deep emotions in God; a deep sadness for what man had become.

10. Anthony A. Hoekema, *Created in God's Image* (Grand Rapids, MI: Eerdmans, 1986), 140–41.

11. D. N. Freedman, A. C. Myers, and A. B. Beck, *Eerdmans Dictionary of the Bible* (Grand Rapids, MI: Eerdmans, 2000), 434.

Chapter 2

1. David Blankenhorn, *Fatherless America* (New York: BasicBooks, 1995), 1.

2. See www.gayparentingmag.com.

3. CENBR/97-1 Issued September 1997 and http://www.census. gov/prod/3/97pubs/cb-9701.pdf.

4. D. N. Freedman, A. C. Myers, and A. B. Beck, *Eerdmans Dictionary of the Bible* (Grand Rapids, MI: Eerdmans, 2000), 456.

5. NET Notes in *The NET Bible First Edition* (Biblical Studies Press, 2006), http://net.bible.org.

6. It is likely that collections of proverbs grew up in the royal courts and were designed for the training of the youthful prince. But once the collection was included in the canon, the term *son* would be expanded to mean a disciple, for all the people were to learn wisdom when young. It would not be limited to sons alone but would include daughters—as the expression "the children of Israel (*béne*)" (including males and females) clearly shows.

7. D. N. Freedman, A. C. Myers, and A. B. Beck, A. B., *Eerdmans Dictionary of the Bible* (Grand Rapids, MI: W.B. Eerdmans, 2000), 456–57.

8. C. Brand, C. Draper, A. England, S. Bond, E. R. Clendenen, T. C Butler, and B. Latta, *Holman Illustrated Bible Dictionary* (Nashville, TN: Holman Bible Publishers, 2003), 3–4.

9. The Greek term *huiothesia* was originally a legal technical term for adoption as a son with full rights of inheritance. BDAG 1024 s.v. notes, "a legal t.t. of 'adoption' of children, in our lit., i.e., in Paul, only in a transferred sense of a transcendent filial relationship between God and humans (with the legal aspect, not gender specificity, as major semantic component)" (NET Notes in *Net Bible*).

10. Even Hebrews states this inferentially that earthly fathers do the best they know how (Heb. 12:10).

11. Peter Scazzero, *Emotionally Healthy Spirituality: Unleash a Revolution in Your Life in Christ* (Kindle Locations 1935–1936).

12. Ibid.

13. J. Swanson, J. *Dictionary of Biblical Languages with Semantic Domains: Hebrew Old Testament* (Oak Harbor: Logos Research Systems, Inc., 1997, electronic edition).

Chapter 3

1. M. G. Easton, *Easton's Bible Dictionary* (Oak Harbor, WA: Logos Research Systems, Inc., 1996).

2. L. Morris, L., *The Epistle to the Romans* (The Pillar New Testament Commentary) (Grand Rapids, MI: Leicester, England: Eerdmans; InterVarsity Press, 1988), 333.

"To be conformed." (Summorphos) In the New Testament it is found again only in Phil. 3:21, where it is followed by the dative. The genitive here is "ablatival" (M, III, p. 215); it means "taking part" etc., here "participating in the form of his image" (BDF 182[1]). And, of course, Christ is in the morphé of God (Phil. 2:6).

"To the likeness." Eixón may denote a literal image or likeness (like the head of the Emperor on a coin), or more generally may mean the form or appearance. Christ is the eixón tou theou (2 Cor. 4:4; Col. 1:15) where "all the emphasis is on the equality of the eixón with the original" (G. Kittel, TDNT, II, p. 395).

3. Oxford Graduate School Dissertation by Carl Ellis, *Thug Spirituality*, from "I Have a Dream" to "Sagging Pants," August 2, 2010, 4.

4. J. B. Green, S. McKnight, and I. H. Marshall, eds, *Dictionary of Jesus and the Gospels* (Downers Grove, IL: InterVarsity Press, 1992), 776.

5. Ibid.

6. M. H. Manser, *Dictionary of Bible Themes: The Accessible and Comprehensive Tool for Topical Studies* (London: Martin Manser, 1999).

7. Donald Macleod, *The Person of Christ* (Downers Grove, IL: InterVarsity Press, 1998), 226.

8. See http://en.wikipedia.org/wiki/Jealousy.

9. See en.wikipedia.org/wiki/jealousy.

10. D. G. Benner and P. C. Hill, eds., *Baker Encyclopedia of Psychology and Counseling* 2nd ed. (Grand Rapids, MI: Baker Books, 1999), 654.

Chapter 4

1. L. Morris, *The Gospel According to John*, The New International Commentary on the New Testament (Grand Rapids, MI: Eerdmans, 1995), 137.

2. Eugene Peterson, *Long Obedience in the Same Direction*, 2nd ed. (Downers Grove, IL: InterVarsity Press, 2000), 17.

3. NET Notes in *The NET Bible First Edition* (Biblical Studies Press, 2000), http://net.bible.org.

4. J. Swanson, J., *Dictionary of Biblical Languages with Semantic Domains: Hebrew Old Testament* (Oak Harbor: Logos Research Systems, Inc., 1997), electronic ed.

5. D. A. Carson, *The Gagging of God* (Grand Rapids: Zondervan, 1996), 47.

6. Charles H. Dunahoo, *Making Kingdom Disciples* (Phillipsburg, NJ: P&R Publishing, 2005), 60.

Chapter 5

1. NET Notes in *The NET Bible First Edition* (Biblical Studies Press, 2006), http://net.bible.org.

2. This passage is a judgment oracle. It announces that conflict between man and woman will become the norm in human society. It does not depict the NT ideal, where the husband sacrificially loves his wife, as Christ loved the church, and where the wife recognizes the husband's loving leadership in the family and voluntarily submits to it. Sin produces a conflict or power struggle between the man and the woman, but in Christ man and woman call a truce and live harmoniously (Eph. 5:18–32).

3. W. A. Elwell, and P. W. Comfort, *Tyndale Bible Dictionary* (Wheaton, IL: Tyndale House Publishers, 2001), 497.

4. "As men fall deeper into the mental habit of fixating on [pornographic images], the exposure to them creates neural pathways. Like

a path is created in the woods with each successive hiker, so do the neural paths set the course for the next time an erotic image is viewed. Over time these neural paths become wider as they are repeatedly traveled with each exposure to pornography. They become the automatic pathway through which interactions with woman are routed. . . . They have unknowingly created a neurological circuit that imprisons their ability to see women rightly as created in God's image" (William M. Struthers, *Wired for Intimacy* [Downers Grove, IL: InterVarsity Press, 2009], 85).

5. See http://www.frc.org/pornography-effects.

6. Source unknown per author.

7. Source unknown per author.

8. NET Notes in *NET Bible* at http://net.bible.org.

9. Thomas Watson, *The Doctrine of Repentance* (Memphis: Bottom of the Hill Publishing, 2012), 15–16.

10. Paul Kruger develops this section as an allegory consisting of a series of metaphors. He suggests that what is at issue is private versus common property. The images of the cistern, well, or fountain are used of a wife (e.g., Song 4:15) because she, like water, satisfies desires. Streams of water in the street would then mean sexual contact with a lewd woman. According to 7:12 she never stays home but is in the streets and is the property of many (P. Kruger, "Promiscuity and Marriage Fidelity? A Note on Prov. 5:15–18, " *JNSL* 13 [1987]: 61–68).

11. The positive instruction is now given: Find pleasure in a fulfilling marriage. The "fountain" is another in the series of implied comparisons with the sexual pleasure that must be fulfilled at home. That it should be blessed (the passive participle of *barakh*) indicates that sexual delight is God-given; having it blessed would mean that it would be endowed with fruitfulness, that it would fulfill all that God intended it to do.

12. Notes in *NET Bible*, http://net.bible.org.

13. W. Arndt, F. W. Danker, and W. Bauer, *A Greek-English Lexicon of the New Testament and Other Early Christian Literature*, 3rd ed. (Chicago: University of Chicago Press, 2000), 254.

14. See http://www.epiphanyfellowship.org/sexandthegospel /recordings.

Chapter 6

1. Jim Cymbala, *Fresh Wind, Fresh Fire* (Grand Rapids: Zondervan, 2008), Kindle edition.

2. NET News in *The NET Bible First Edition* (Biblical Studies Press, 2006), http://net.bible.org.

3. John Gray, *Men Are from Mars, Women Are from Venus: Practical Guide for Improving Communication* (New York: HarperCollins, Inc., 2009), Kindle edition, 26.

4. NET Notes in *NET Bible*, http://net.bible.org.

5. W. A. Elwell, and B. J. Beitzel, *Baker Encyclopedia of the Bible* (Grand Rapids: Baker Book House, 1988), 2149.

6. NET notes in *Net Bible. Heb* "no vision." The Hebrew word *vision* (from the verb *khazah*, "to see") refers to divine communication to prophets (as in 1 Sam. 3:1) and not to individual goals or plans. C. H. Toy sees a problem here: The most calamitous period of Israel's history was when prophetic vision was at its height, whereas people were often more obedient when God was silent. He also notes that in the book of Proverbs there is no mention of prophetic teaching with wisdom as a guide. So he emends the word to "guidance" following the LXX (*Proverbs* [ICC], 512). The TEV has "guidance"; the NIV retains "revelation." It must be stated that the prophetic ministry was usually in response to the calamitous periods, calling the people back to God. Without them, the downward rush to anarchy and destruction would have been faster than with these prophetic calls from God.

7. Andy Stanley, *Visioneering* (Colorado Springs: Multnomah Books, 1999), 8.

8. Ibid., 9–11, taken from various statements.

9. J. Swanson, *Dictionary of Biblical Languages with Semantic Domains: Hebrew Old Testament* (Oak Harbor: Logos Research Systems, Inc., 1997), electronic edition.

10. NET Notes in *NET Bible*, http://net.bible.org.

11. J. Swanson, *Dictionary of Biblical Languages*.

12. R. L. Harris, G. L. Archer, Jr. and B. K. Waltke, eds., *Theological Wordbook of the Old Testament* (Chicago: Moody Press, 1999), electronic ed., 970.

13. Garry Friesen, *Decision Making and the Will of God* (Colorado Springs: Multnomah Book, 2004), 271–72.

14. NET Notes in *NET Bible*, http://net.bible.org.

15. Friesen, *Decision Making*, 271.

Chapter 7

1. The aorist active form is used of a particular time in the past as a snapshot picture whereby Jesus positionally cleansed the wife.

2. T. Friberg, B. Friberg, and N. F. Miller, *Analytical Lexicon of the Greek New Testament*, vol. 4 (Grand Rapids: Baker Books, 2000), 194.

3. Ibid., 55.

4. See http://www.bet.com/news/celebrities/2011/11/18/jay-z -opens-up-about-relationship-with-his-father.html.

5. W. Arndt, F. W. Danker, and W. Bauer, *A Greek-English Lexicon of the New Testament and Other Early Christian Literature*, 3rd ed. (Chicago: University of Chicago Press 2000), 986.

6. P. H. Towner, *The Letters to Timothy and Titus: The New International Commentary on the New Testament* (Grand Rapids: Eerdmans Publishing, 2006), 730–31.

7. W. Arndt, F. W. Danker, and W. Bauer, *A Greek-English Lexicon of the New Testament*, 919.

8. W. D. Mounce, *Pastoral Epistles*, vol. 46, *Word Biblical Commentary* (Dallas: Word, Incorporated, 2000), 409.

9. Arndt, Danker, and Bauer, *A Greek-English Lexicon of the New Testament*, 919.

10. "*Gray hair* is a metonymy of adjunct; it represents everything valuable about old age—dignity, wisdom, honor, experience, as well as worry and suffering of life. At the very least, since they survived, they must know something. At the most, they were the sages and elders of the people" (NET Notes in *NET Bible*, http://net.bible.org).

11. Arndt, Danker, and Bauer, *A Greek-English Lexicon of the New Testament*, 1039.

12. J. H. Walton, *Zondervan Illustrated Bible Backgrounds Commentary (Old Testament) Volume 5: The Minor Prophets, Job, Psalms, Proverbs, Ecclesiastes, Song of Songs* (Grand Rapids: Zondervan, 2009), 426.

13. NET Notes in *NET Bible*, http://net.bible.org.

14. Ibid.

15. Dr. Thomas Constable's *Notes on Psalms*, 2000 edition, 194.

Chapter 8

1. David Murrow, *Why Do Men Hate Going to Church?* (Nashville: Thomas Nelson, 2011). See http://churchformen.com/men-and-church /why-do-men-hate-going-to-church.

2. Thomas Watson, *The Godly Man's Picture* (Carlisle, PA: Banner of Truth, 1992, 61–62.

3. τοὺς ἄνδρας (accusative plural as "subject" of the infinitive) means "men" here in distinction from women, as the use of γυναῖκας in the next verse implies. This distinction is borne out by the usage elsewhere in the PE* (1 Tim. 2:8, 12; 3:2, 12; 5:9; Titus 1:6; 2:5). The plural (which seems to point beyond individual homes and families), coupled with the possible nuance of the following prepositional phrase and the wider context in vv. 1, 11, 12 (learning, teaching, exercising authority) and 3:14, 15 ("that you may know how one ought to conduct himself in the household of God"), all seem to point to public prayer by more than one individual in church gatherings. Men are specified here because it is their particular responsibility to lead the church and its worship service (cf. v. 12; 3:2, 5; 4:11–16; 5:17). Paul thus gives specific instructions to men here just as he will give specific instructions to women in the verses that follow (vv. 9ff.).

4. P. Towner, *1–2 Timothy & Titus*, vol. 14, *The IVP New Testament Commentary Series* (Downers Grove, IL: InterVarsity Press, 1994), 1 Tim. 2:8.

5. P. C. Craigie, *Psalms 1–50*, vol. 19, *Word Biblical Commentary* (Dallas: Word, Inc., 1998), 232.

6. W. Arndt, F. W. Danker, and W. Bauer, *A Greek-English Lexicon of the New Testament and Other Early Christian Literature*, 3rd ed. (Chicago: University of Chicago Press, 2000), 765.

7. Larry Kreider, *The Cry for Spiritual Fathers and Mothers* (Ephrata, PA: House to House Pub., 2000), 38.

8. Paramutheomai (comfort) in L. Coenen, E. Beyreuther, and H. Bietenhard, eds., *New International Dictionary of New Testament Theology*, vol. 2 (Grand Rapids: Zondervan Publishing House, 1986), 329.

9. T. Friberg, B. Friberg, and N. F. Miller, *Analytical Lexicon of the Greek New Testament*, vol. 4 (Grand Rapids: Baker Books, 2000), 254.

SCRIPTURE INDEX